Stimulus Equivalence for Students with Developmental Disabilities

Stimulus Equivalence for Students with Developmental Disabilities provides a step-by-step program for converting lesson plans into equivalence-based instruction. Using language and tools accessible to both students and practitioners, chapters present the concept of equivalence-based instruction and include clear and concise procedural descriptions, as well as data sheets and PowerPoint slides, with replaceable stimuli, so that special educators and clinicians will be able to immediately implement this procedure to teach any academic skill. Written in engaging prose with an emphasis on practical application, this book is an essential resource for special educators and graduate students studying to become BCBAs and special educators.

Russell W. Maguire is Associate Professor, Behavior Analysis, Simmons University, US.

Ronald F. Allen is Associate Professor of Practice and Director of the Doctoral Program for Behavior Analysis at Simmons University, US.

T0386345

Stimulus Equivalence for Students with Developmental Disabilities

A Practical Guide to Equivalence-Based Instruction

Edited by
Russell W. Maguire and Ronald F. Allen

Routledge
Taylor & Francis Group

NEW YORK AND LONDON

Cover image: Russell W. Maguire and Ronald F. Allen

First published 2023
by Routledge
605 Third Avenue, New York, NY 10158

and by Routledge
4 Park Square, Milton Park, Abingdon, Oxon, OX14 4RN

Routledge is an imprint of the Taylor & Francis Group, an informa business

Library of Congress Cataloging-in-Publication Data
Names: Maguire, Russell W., editor. | Allen, Ronald F., editor.
Title: Stimulus equivalence for students with developmental disabilities:
    a practical guide to equivalence-based instruction / edited by Russell
    W. Maguire and Ronald F. Allen.
Description: New York, NY : Routledge, 2023. | Includes bibliographical
    references and index.
Identifiers: LCCN 2022020402 (print) | LCCN 2022020403 (ebook) |
    ISBN 9781032285207 (hardback) | ISBN 9781032282138 (paperback) |
    ISBN 9781003297161 (ebook)
Subjects: LCSH: Developmentally disabled children—Education. | Thought and
    thinking—Study and teaching. | Special education—Curricula. | Lesson
    planning.
Classification: LCC LC4661 .S76 2023 (print) | LCC LC4661 (ebook) | DDC
    371.9/043—dc23/eng/20220707
LC record available at https://lccn.loc.gov/2022020402
LC ebook record available at https://lccn.loc.gov/2022020403

ISBN: 978-1-032-28520-7 (hbk)
ISBN: 978-1-032-28213-8 (pbk)
ISBN: 978-1-003-29716-1 (ebk)

DOI: 10.4324/9781003297161

Typeset in Palatino
by Apex CoVantage, LLC

Contents

Contributors

Ronald F. Allen is faculty in the Department of Behavior Analysis at Simmons University and a Board Certified Behavior Analyst (BACB-D), Simmons University, USA.

Megan Breault is a licensed BCBA in Boston, Massachusetts who works as a Clinical Director for an in-home ABA therapy agency and an adjunct faculty at Simmons University Simmons University, USA.

Christina M. King, Ph.D., BCBA, LABA, is Associate Professor of Practice in the Behavior Analysis Online Program at Simmons University, Simmons University, USA.

Emily Leonard is a third grade teacher in Massachusetts. She possesses a PhD in Behavior Analysis from Simmons College and she is Board Certified Behavior Analyst (BACB-D), Simmons University and Brookline, MA, Public Schools, USA.

Russell W. Maguire is faculty in the Department of Behavior Analysis at Simmons University and a Board Certified Behavior Analyst (BACB-D), Simmons University, USA.

Simone Palmer possesses Masters and Doctoral degrees and has more than 15 years' experience working with children with developmental disabilities. She is also a Board Certified Behavior Analyst-Doctoral (BCBA-D) and a Licensed Applied Behavior Analyst (LABA), Simmons University and Bierman Autism Centers, USA

Colleen Yorlets specializes in working with children with autism and is interested in the topics of stimulus control, stimulus equivalence, and verbal behavior. Simmons University, USA.

Preface

Stimulus Equivalence and Equivalence-Based Instruction (EBI) are little known terms outside of the field of Behavior Analysis. Each of the contributors of this book (as well as all equivalence researchers) often wonder, "Why isn't EBI in every classroom in America?" However, this failure to embrace EBI by the Educational Community has nothing to do with the lack of scientific validity of stimulus equivalence, but rather everything to do with the challenge of providing educators with evidence of the profound efficacy of EBI in a digestible form. This book is one attempt at overcoming that challenge.

This book is not to be a source of new theoretical insights for researchers of derived relational responding. Such questions are beyond the scope of this book. Instead, this book hopes to provide a step-by-step program for converting lesson plans into EBI teaching (along with a dash of science for validation). We also hope to provide structure and materials (e.g., clear and simple data sheets) for teachers to ease the curriculum modifications inherent in any new instructional format. The good news is, with a little up-front work, the educational outcomes for your students will be enormous.

Thanks for reading and thanks for the work you do.

RWM/RA

1

Introduction to Stimulus Equivalence and Equivalence-Based Instruction

Russell W. Maguire and Ronald F. Allen

What is a Concept?

According to (Parker (2018), "a concept is defined by the critical character-istics shared by all examples of the concept," and "for something to be an example of a concept it must contain all these critical characteristics" (p. 1). For example, the concept of "redness" may include different shades of red (e.g., different wavelengths) yet each wavelength shares some characteristic of "redness." If taught well, the learner may then classify novel, untaught wavelengths as belonging to the class of red, if those wavelengths possess the relevant physical properties of redness. Consequently, humans may form concepts or classify stimuli based on their physical similarities.

However, Jonassen (2006) indicated that concepts or classes may also form in the absence of shared physical characteristics, based on rules of inclu-sion. For example, the concept of dogs may include physically dissimilar items, such as a picture of a dog, the printed word D-O-G and the spoken word "dog." Although most would agree that these items are related to one another, their inclusion within this concept is not based on shared physical characteristics. Thus, concepts or classes may form based on physicality and/or shared rules of inclusion.

Layng (2017) expanded on the idea of a concept by stating that items belonging to any concept must include *must-have features* and then may also

DOI: 10.4324/9781003297161-1

include *can-have features*. So, using the dog concept, *must have features* may include four legs, a tail and barking whereas *can have features* may be different types of fur (e.g., long, short, none), size (e.g., small, large) or physical resemblance, or not, to a wolf. Unfortunately, for this idea of a concept to be functional there must be agreement as to *must have features*, not an easy thing in education today.

Perhaps a better definition of concept is the one that does not rely, exclusively, on either shared physical properties or rules of inclusion. Keller and Schoenfeld (1950) indicated that if items are followed by the same response (e.g., saying dog when one hears the spoken word "dog" or when one sees an actual dog) then they are members of the same class (e.g., concept). Keller and Schoenfeld (1950) described what has been termed stimulus classes (Cooper et al., 2020).

Regardless, teaching to the formation of such classes, instead of focusing on isolated, discrete skills, may accelerate learning and also allow learners to include in the class novel items that they encounter outside of their learning: for example, the above example that illustrated the concept of redness, based on what is called primary stimulus generalization (Cooper et al., 2020) or multiple exemplar training (Holth, 2017). According to this account, novel items that share physical similarities with trained items may become members of the same class (concept) after exposure to some number of multiple examples displaying those physical similarities. So, after teaching a number of different pictures of different shades of red (multiple exemplars), the learner may include novel wavelengths of red as members of the class/concept, without being taught to do so. Unfortunately, primary stimulus generalization or multiple exemplar training has some downsides as an instructional approach. For example:

- ◆ just how many examples are required for one to form a concept is unknown;
- ◆ items that should be members of a class may not be perceived by the learner as sharing critical physical characteristics or satisfying the rules of inclusion;
- ◆ items that should not be members of a class may be perceived by the learner as sharing critical physical characteristics or satisfying the rules of inclusion (e.g., a goat may be included in the class of dogs because it has four legs, a tail and does something akin to barking).

As the reader can see, teaching via multiple exemplar training may not be applicable for all classes, especially those that include physically different items. Unfortunately, this approach, in which prior learning is thought to set the occasion for future learning, has been the primary mode of instruction in education today (Wexler, 2019). What is needed is a new definition of a concept and a more effective way to teach concepts. A behavioral definition of concept, or class, based on the findings of stimulus equivalence research (Sidman & Tailby, 1982; Sidman, 1994) addresses these issues. An example may prove illustrative.

Keisha is an 11-year-old girl with learning challenges who experiences difficulty with basic geometry. Her teacher, who is also a Board Certified Behavior Analyst (BCBA), decided to teach Keisha geometry via equivalence-based instruction. First, a pretest was administered to determine which geometric concepts Keisha did and did not know. The results determined that Keisha could not accurately:

- select a geometric form or its definition when the teacher said "Touch _____" (the name of the form);
- match a form to its definition;
- match a definition to its form;
- name each form and definition.

Given these findings Keisha was first taught to select a rhombus or a trapezoid or a rectangle, on alternate trials, when the teacher said, "Touch rhombus or trapezoid or rectangle." Of course, correct selections were reinforced, creating relations between the *specific* spoken word/name ("rhombus," "trapezoid," "rectangle") and the *specific* corresponding visual form (rhombus, trapezoid, rectangle), respectively. Figure 1.1 presents a diagram of a typical instructional trial.

After acquiring these three skills (e.g., spoken word-to-form for the three different geometric forms) Keisha was taught, again within a discrete trial format, to select a definition of a rhombus or a trapezoid or a rectangle, again on alternating trials, when the teacher said "Touch rhombus or trapezoid or rectangle." The following diagram presents this instruction.

Again, correct selections were reinforced, creating relations between the *specific* spoken word/name ("rhombus," "trapezoid," "rectangle") and the

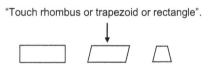

"Touch rhombus or trapezoid or rectangle".

Figure 1.1 Training Trial Illustrating Matching Forms to Their Corresponding Spoken Names.

"Touch rhombus or trapezoid or rectangle"

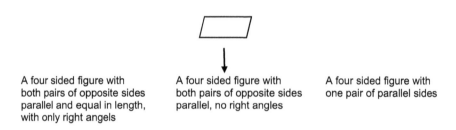

| A four sided figure with both pairs of opposite sides parallel and equal in length, with only right angles | A four sided figure with both pairs of opposite sides parallel, no right angles | A four sided figure with one pair of parallel sides |

Figure 1.2 Training Trial Illustrating Matching Printed Word Definitions to Their Corresponding Spoken Names.

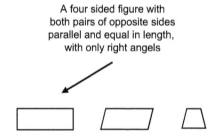

| A four sided figure with both pairs of opposite sides parallel and equal in length, with only right angels | A four sided figure with both pairs of opposite sides parallel, no right angles | A four sided figure with one pair of parallel sides |

Figure 1.3 Training Trial Illustrating Matching Printed Word Definitions to Their Corresponding Forms

A four sided figure with
both pairs of opposite sides
parallel and equal in length,
with only right angels

Figure 1.4 Training Trial Illustrating Matching Forms to Their Corresponding Printed Word Definitions.

specific corresponding printed word definition (rhombus, trapezoid, rectangle), respectively.

Please note that the forms and the printed definitions were now both directly related to the spoken word and, as a result, *perhaps indirectly to each other*.

Following these two teachings, a posttest, similar to the pretest, was conducted. First, a form appeared as the sample. On these trials, Keisha was to select the printed word definition that "matched" the form. Figure 1.3 presents an example of this test trial arrangement.

On other trials, the printed word definition served as the sample. On these occasions Keisha was to select the form that "matched" the definition. Figure 1.4 presents an example of this test trial arrangement.

Further, a form or a printed word definition was presented alone and Keisha was asked "What is this?" and she was to name the form or a printed word definition.

Finally, Keisha was given twenty-four cards consisting of eight novel rhombi, trapezoids and rectangles (different sizes, colors and orientations) and asked to put them into groups that "*go together*." It is important to emphasize that Keisha had never seen these twenty-four forms before.

Keisha's responses on the test trials revealed that she related forms to printed-word definitions (and vice versa), named forms, and printed word definitions and grouped novel forms, without error, consistent with the concepts rhombus, trapezoid and rectangle. *Keisha demonstrated all these skills even though they had not been taught.*

As a consequence Keisha formed three classes, or concepts (rhombus, trapezoid and rectangle) each consisting of a spoken word, a visual form and a printed definition plus the additional, never-before-seen forms for each concept. Keisha demonstrated *four new untrained skills* for each concept for *every two skills taught*. Across the three concepts, Keisha was taught *six skills* and *twelve new skills emerged without ever having been taught*. Although this is a hypothetical example, it is based on an actual study conducted by Sumner et al. (2010).

Keisha formed concepts/classes that involved 1) items (stimuli) that shared no physical similarities and 2) other items that did share physical characteristics. What rules (Jonassen, 2006) were in play that can account for the formation of such classes? According to Sidman (2000) the physically different academic items became related to one another and formed a class (concept) because of how the teaching occurred. Two of the three items within each class were directly related to one another through teaching and reinforcement. *Because the two different visual items (e.g., forms and definitions) were directly related to the spoken word, all three became related to one another.* Behaviorally speaking, this phenomenon has been called stimulus equivalence (Sidman, 1971; Sidman & Tailby, 1982). Additionally, the inclusion of the novel forms in the classes/concepts, based on physical similarities, has been called "generalized equivalence classes" (Adams et al., 1993a).

Since 1971, when the first account of equivalence was published by Sidman, studies evaluating stimulus equivalence have reported reliably effective and consistently economic findings (Ayres-Pereira & Arntzen, 2021; Fields et al., 1984; Hall & Chase, 1991; Maguire et al., 1994; Rehfeldt, 2011; Saunders & Green, 1999; Sidman, 1994; Sidman, 2000; Sidman, 2009). The specifics of this research will not be recounted here but suffice it to say that there is a substantial body of experimental literature supporting the stimulus equivalence account.

Additionally, these experimental findings have been replicated when applied to academic instruction (i.e., "equivalence-based instruction," EBI, Fienup & Critchfield, 2011). Rehfeldt (2011) reviewed studies investigating stimulus equivalence published from 1992 through 2009. This review cited twenty-six studies and included individuals with developmental disabilities and children with learning challenges as participants. Pilgrim (2016) reported that since 1982 over 500 studies were published in the *Journal of the Experimental Analysis of Behavior* citing "stimulus equivalence", as keywords. Brodsky and Fienup (2018) conducted a meta-analysis on the application of equivalence-based instruction involving college content and found twenty-eight studies published between March 2016 and August 2016 documenting the effectiveness of equivalence-based instruction. More specifically, a variety of academic skills have been taught via equivalence-based instruction to children with developmental disabilities and autism-spectrum disorders. The following list details a small sampling of this research:

◆ geography (LeBlanc et al., 2003);
◆ reading comprehension (Sidman, 1971; Groskreutz et al, 2010; Lane & Critchfield, 1998; Mackay, 1985; Sidman & Cresson, 1973);
◆ geometry (Dixon et al., 2016)
◆ functional money skills (McDonagh et al., 1984; Keintz et al., 2011).

So, given this history, why isn't equivalence-based instruction a standard classroom educational intervention? There may be a number of reasons for this. First, Critchfield (2018) noted that the transition from laboratory investigations to classroom application is typically a slow process.

Second, Begeny and Martens (2006) reported that students training to become regular and special education teachers received little training in behavioral protocols, especially in the areas of instructional programming. Unfortunately, this finding appears to have continued to the present day. In a recent issue of *Teaching Exceptional Children*, Pennington (2018) reported "Despite its pervasive impact on the provision of services to students with disabilities, educators may still be unfamiliar with ABA [applied behavior analysis]" (p. 319). This author also suggested that special educators may possess misperceptions of behavioral interventions, which may further interfere with the application of these efficacious interventions.

Third, equivalence-based protocols can be complex, given the requirements for training and testing and the technical terminology. Critchfield (2018) indicated that much of the published stimulus-equivalence literature involves esoteric language and procedures that even trained behavior analysts may find daunting. Thus, even if a special educator possessed knowledge regarding behavior analytic instructional protocols, knowledge of EBI is probably beyond what was taught in graduate school.

Fourth, in addition to unfamiliar terms and protocols, equivalence-based protocols can be complex and time consuming, given the requirements for training and testing (Palmer et al., 2021). As Critchfield (2018) reported, "training procedures. . . can be quite effortful to devise. Although the yield of learning is great, the behavioral engineer's up-front investment can be sizeable" (p. 208). Consequently, the special educator, or behavior analyst, may default to other, less effective, although easier to use, interventions than EBI.

Purpose

The primary purpose of this book is to describe the EBI procedure in a manner that is devoid of technical jargon so that it is easily understood and can be immediately implemented by classroom personnel. The hope is that by doing so equivalence-based protocols will be used more frequently as a standard classroom instructional procedure.

To this end, the book is broken down in the following way:

Chapter 1 presents a typical and somewhat ambiguous educational definition of a concept, contrasted with a more objective behavioral stimulus-equivalence account of concepts. Chapter 1 also highlights the application of equivalence-based instruction (EBI) to academics by providing an example of teaching geometry concepts and ending with the potential barriers to using EBI in the classroom;

Chapter 2 reviews, defines and explains the jargon typically associated with EBI (e.g., discrete trial training, matching-to-sample, simple and conditional discriminations, and the properties of equivalence). This chapter also reviews Sidman's seminal 1971 study and the procedures, as well as their sequence, typically required for EBI;

Chapter 3 presents the potential disadvantages of conducting testing for the emergence of classes of equivalent stimuli (e.g., excessive number of trials, the time and effort needed to prepare for the administration of tests, the absence of feedback during testing) and a time- and labor-saving alternative (sorting);

Chapter 4 provides an overview of the requirements for pretesting, teaching, and conducting posttests within an EBI approach. This approach uses sorting for pretesting, conducting posttests, and matching-to-sample/discrete trials for teaching;

Chapter 5 presents an option to enhance the already efficient EBI process (e.g., using multi-element items) and also the use of errorless instruction;

Chapter 6 offers the use of differential outcomes (e.g., specific reinforcers restricted to each specific class) as a method used during instruction, to increase the probability of the emergence of classes of equivalent items following teaching;

Chapter 7 explores the relationship between the emergence of language (e.g., verbal behavior) and stimulus equivalence and how this relation may be used to enhance language acquisition of individuals with developmental disabilities;

Chapter 8 reviews three applied studies teaching a child with an autism-spectrum disorder, neuro-typical kindergarten, and third-grade-students science concepts via EBI;

Finally, Chapter 9 provides a step-by-step sequence for pretesting, teaching, and conducting posttests using an EBI approach. The chapter, and the book, ends with a "lesson plan" that may guide a classroom teacher in the development and implementation of an EBI program.

References

Adams, B. J., Fields, L., & Verhave, T. (1993a). Effects of test order on inter-subject variability during equivalence class formation. *The Psychological Record*, *43*, 133–152.

Ayres-Pereira, V., & Arntzen, E. (2021). A descriptive analysis of baseline and equivalence-class performances under many-to-one and one-to-many structures. *Journal of the Experimental Analysis of Behavior*, *115*, 540–560. https://doi.org/10.1002/jeab.678

Begeny, J. C., & Martens, B. K. (2006). Assessing pre-service teachers' training in empirically-validated behavioral instruction practices. *School Psychology Quarterly*, *21*, 262–285. https://doi.org/10.1521/scpq.2006.21.3.262

Brodsky, J., & Fienup, D. M. (2018). Sidman goes to college: A meta-analysis of equivalence-based instruction in higher education. *Perspectives on Behavior Science*, *41*, 95–119. https://doi.org/10.1007/s40614-018-0150-0

Cooper, J. O., Heron, T. E., & Heward, W. L. (2020). *Applied behavior analysis* (3rd ed.). Pearson Education.

Critchfield, T. S. (2018). Efficiency is everything: Promoting efficient practice by harnessing derived stimulus relations. *Behavior Analysis in Practice*, *11*, 206–210. https://doi.org/10.1007/s40617-018-0262-8

Dixon, M. R., Belisle, J., Stanley, C. R., Daar, J. H., & Williams, L. A. (2016). Derived equivalence relations of geometry skills in students with autism: An application of the PEAK-E curriculum. *The Analysis of Verbal Behavior, 32*, 45-. https://doi.org/10.1007/s40616-016-0051-9. PMID: 27606220; PMCID: PMC488355

Fields, L., Verhave, T., & Fath, S. (1984). Stimulus equivalence and transitive associations: A methodological analysis. *Journal of the Experimental Analysis of Behavior, 42*, 143–157. https://doi.org/10.1901/jeab.1984.42-143

Fienup, D. M., & Critchfield, T. S. (2011). Transportability of equivalence-based programmed instruction: Efficacy and efficiency in a college classroom. *Journal of Applied Behavior Analysis, 44*, 435–450. https://doi.org/10.1901/jaba.2011.44-435

Groskreutz, N. C., Karsina, A., Miguel, C. F., & Groskreutz, M. P. (2010). Using complex auditory-visual samples to produce emergent relations in children with autism. *Journal of Applied Behavior analysis, 43*, 131–136. https://doi.org/10.1901/jaba.2010.43-131

Hall, G. A., & Chase, P. N. (1991). The relationship between stimulus equivalence and verbal behavior. *The Analysis of Verbal Behavior, 9*, 107–119. https://doi.org/10.1007/BF03392865

Holth P. (2017). Multiple exemplar training: Some strengths and limitations. *The Behavior Analyst, 40*, 225–241. https://doi.org/10.1007/s40614-017-0083-z

Jonassen, D. H. (2006). On the role of concepts in learning and instructional design *Educational Technology Research and Development, 54*, 177–196.

Keintz, K. S., Miguel, C. F., Kao, B., & Finn, H. E. (2011). Using conditional discrimination training to produce emergent relations between coins and their values in children with autism. *Journal of the Applied Behavior Analysis, 44*, 909–913. https://doi.org/10.1901/jaba.2011.44-909

Keller, F. S., & Schoenfeld, W. N. (1950). *Principles of psychology.* Appleton-Century-Crofts.

Lane, S. D., & Critchfield, T. S. (1998). Increasing the generativity of identity-based procedures for establishing arbitrary conditional relations. *The Psychological Record, 48*, 457–479.

Layng, T. V. J. (2017). Understanding concepts: Implications for science teaching. (In progress)

LeBlanc, L. A., Miguel, C. F., Cummings, A. R., Goldsmith, T. R., & Carr, J. E. (2003). The effects of three stimulus-equivalence testing conditions on emergent US geography relations of children diagnosed with autism. *Behavioral Interventions: Theory & Practice in Residential & Community-Based Clinical Programs, 18*, 279–289. https://doi.org/10.1002/bin.144

Mackay, H. A. (1985). Stimulus equivalence in rudimentary reading and spelling. *Analysis and Intervention in Developmental Disabilities*, *5*, 373–387. https://doi.org/10.1016/0270-4684(85)90006-0

Maguire, R. W., Stromer, R., Mackay, H. A., & Demis, C. A. (1994). Matching to complex samples and stimulus class formation in adults with autism and young children. *Journal of Autism and Developmental Disorders*, *24*, 753–772. https://doi.org/10.1007/BF02172284

McDonagh, E. C., McIlvane, W. J., & Stoddard, L. T. (1984). Teaching coin equivalences via matching to sample. *Applied Research in Mental Retardation*, *5*, 177–197.

Palmer, S. K., Maguire, R. W., Lionello-DeNolf, K., & Braga-Kenyon, P. (2021). The inclusion of prompts in equivalence classes. *Journal of the Experimental Analysis of Behavior*, *115*(1), 255–271.

Parker, W. (2018). https://teachinghistory.org/teaching-materials/teaching-guides/25184

Pennington, R. (2018). Special issue on behavior analysis in education. *Teaching Exceptional Children*, *50*, 319–320. https://doi.org/10.1177/0040059918776161

Pilgrim, C. (2016). Considering definitions of stimulus equivalence. *European Journal of Behavior Analysis*, *17*, 1–10. https://doi.org/10.1080/15021149.2016.1156312

Rehfeldt, R. A. (2011). Toward a technology of derived stimulus relations: An analysis of articles published in the Journal of Applied Behavior Analysis, 1992–2009. *Journal of Applied Behavior Analysis*, *44*, 109–119. https://doi.org/10.1901/jaba.2011.44-109

Saunders, R. R., & Green, G. (1999). A discrimination analysis of training-structure effects on stimulus equivalence outcomes. *Journal of the Experimental Analysis of Behavior*, *72*, 117–137. https://doi.org/10.1901/jeab.1999.72-117

Sidman, M. (1971). Reading and auditory-visual equivalences. *Journal of Speech and Hearing Research*, *14*, 5–13. https://doi.org/10.1044/jshr.1401.05

Sidman, M. (1994) *Equivalence relations and behavior: A research story*. Authors Cooperative. ISBN-13:978–0962331169

Sidman, M. (2000). Equivalence relations and the reinforcement contingency. *Journal of the Experimental Analysis of Behavior*, *74*, 127–146. https://doi.org/10.1901/jeab.2000.74-127

Sidman, M. (2009). Equivalence relations and behavior: An introductory tutorial. *The Analysis of Verbal Behavior*, *25*, 5–17. https://doi.org/10.1007/BF03393066

Sidman, M., & Cresson, O. (1973). Reading and crossmodal transfer of stimulus equivalences in severe retardation. *American Journal of Mental Deficiency*, *77*, 515–523.

Sidman, M., & Tailby, W. (1982). Conditional discrimination vs. matching to sample: An expansion of the testing paradigm. *Journal of the Experimental Analysis of Behavior*, *37*, 5–22. https://doi.org/10.1901/jeab.1982.37-5

Sumner, C., Maguire, R. W., & Cameron, M. J. (2010). The formation of geometric equivalences following group instruction. In R. W. Maguire (Chair) *Educational applications of stimulus equivalence methodology*. Paper presented at the 36th Annual Convention of the Association of Behavior Analysis, International, San Antonio, Texas.

Wexler, N. (2019). Elementary education has gone terribly wrong. *The Atlantic*.

2

Definition, History and Brief Overview of Stimulus Equivalence and Equivalence-Based Instruction

Russell W. Maguire and Ronald F. Allen

Science creates its own language. It does so in order for the investigators within any particular field to discuss their findings with colleagues in a precise and cogent manner. But in doing so, the jargon that develops often excludes the very people who could make good, applied use of the interventions being discussed. As noted in Chapter 1, this may be one reason why EBI has not been widely embraced in the classroom, despite its robust results. What follows is an attempt to "pull back the curtain" and explain critical terms and procedures in everyday language. Thus, the "jargon" will be presented, followed by what is hoped to be understandable explanations, in everyday language.

Discrete Trial Training

Discrete trial training (DTT) is a time-honored behavior analytic teaching protocol, especially for the instruction of students with developmental disabilities (Dib & Sturmey, 2007; Lerman et al., 2016). However, it must be noted that this methodology has been successful as well with neuro-typical

DOI: 10.4324/9781003297161-2

individuals (Higbee et al., 2016). DTT grew out of the more sophisticated laboratory methodology, matching-to-sample (MTS). Regardless, for the remainder of this text the terms DTT and MTS will be used and described synonymously.

When using DTT/MTS, students are typically presented a number of items as choices or comparisons (e.g., words, numbers, pictures, etc.) and are taught to select the correct choice or comparison, either based on some teacher direction or a sample to be matched. This can be accomplished in one of two ways: teaching simple discriminations (i.e., three-term contingencies) or teaching conditional discriminations (e.g., four-term contingencies). Each will be discussed in turn.

Simple Discriminations

One may use DTT/MTS to teach a simple discrimination or a three-term contingency. A three-term contingency consists of a correct choice as **the first term (antecedent)**, the behavior to be taught as **the second term (behavior)**, and the consequence as **the third term (consequence)**. In this arrangement, the correct choice is the same item on every trial and, over time, its mere presence comes to control and cue the desired behavior, assuming the consequence is reinforcing. A few examples may prove helpful, listed in Table 2.1. First, when driving you happen upon a stop sign (**antecedent**). In its presence you stop (**behavior**) because the **consequence** may be avoiding an accident or a ticket. Note that every stop sign exerts this level of control over your stopping behavior, even if it is a novel stop sign or you are in an unfamiliar location. The reason that the antecedent, in this case the stop sign, reliably controls behavior is because of the history of stopping at stop sign reliably produces a desired outcome (e.g., avoiding an accident and/or ticket). This history is akin to teaching a student a new skill.

Table 2.1 Examples of Simple Discriminations (Three-Term Contingencies)

First Term (Antecedent)	Second Term (Behavior)	Third Term (Consequence)
Stop Sign Color Red Telephone Ring	Stop Touch Answer	Avoid an Accident Correct Response: Praise Talk to a Friend

A teaching example is illustrative. Assume that students are taught that the color red is always the correct choice and selecting this color is always reinforced (Figure 2.1). The comparisons are presented, which is also the "cue" for the student to respond (Figure 2.1). Regardless of the placement of the color red (e.g., left, middle, right) it is always the correct choice. Selecting red produces reinforcement whereas selecting any other color does not.

A final example is when your telephone rings (**first term: antecedent**), you answer it (**second term: behavior**) and if the **consequence** is positive, such as talking with a friend, you are more likely to answer your telephone in the future. Table 2.1 provides examples of a three-term contingency.

One might ask, "Why would one teach a student that the color red is always the correct choice when, often, it is not?" In this case, the color red, once trained, could be used as an extra stimulus prompt during the instruction of new skills (see Chapter 5 for an expanded discussion of extra stimulus prompts and errorless instruction). During teaching, any new correct choice could be highlighted in red, signaling to the student that it was the correct choice. Over trials, the red color could be systematically faded out, transferring "correctness" from the color red to the item itself.

Conditional Discriminations

Often, these three-term contingencies come under the control of a different, fourth element. If this happens, the previously three-term contingencies become four-term contingencies or conditional discriminations. Table 2.2 provides examples of four-term contingencies (conditional discriminations) based on the three-term contingencies, listed in Table 2.1.

Suppose as you approach a stop sign there is a police officer and she waves you on (i.e., to not stop). If you follow the officer's direction to drive through the stop sign you will avoid being reprimanded by the officer for not complying. Notice that the previous, highly reliable control exerted by the stop sign now is conditional upon the presence (or absence) of the police officer (Table 2.2).

Figure 2.1 Examples of Three-Term Contingency

Table 2.2 Examples of Conditional Discriminations (Four-Term Contingencies)

Fourth Term (Conditional Stimulus)	First Term (Discriminative Stimulus)	Second Term (Behavior)	Third Term (Consequence)
Police Officer "Touch Red" In or Out of Class	Stop Sign Color Red Telephone Ring	Comply with Officer Touch Answer or Not	Avoid Reprimand Correct: Praise Talk to a Friend

What if a teacher wants to bring students' selection of the color red, as well as other colors, under the control of the spoken direction "Touch red or green or blue" (Table 2.2)? This turns the three-term contingency, discussed above, into a four-term contingency with the new, fourth term being the teacher's spoken direction. Thus, the student's selection of a color, red or green or blue, is now "conditional" on the specific teacher's direction (e.g., touch red or green or blue).

Finally, assume that your telephone rings when you are in class versus when you are not in class. Whether or not you answer your telephone is "conditional" upon where you are. If in class, you will refrain from answering your telephone, whereas you may answer if you are somewhere that behavior is appropriate.

Four-term contingencies are also known as conditional discriminations, because the correct choice is **contingent, or conditional**, upon the fourth term, as presented in Table 2.2 and explained previously.

Figure 2.2 provides a schematic of teaching selection of a color when the fourth term is the teacher's direction "Touch _____" (a color), or to touch the color that relates to a printed word, or that matches an identical sample (the fourth term).

It is important to emphasize that the fourth term can be auditory (e.g., a spoken word or direction, as described above) or any other modality (e.g., visual, olfactory, tactile, etc.).

Also, note that during instruction of simple and conditional discriminations the placement of comparisons (in this case, colors) each appear to the student equally often in the left, right and middle positions in an unpredictable manner. This is to avoid the creation of a position bias that may confound instruction.

In conditional discriminations, **the first term** is the sample, also called the *conditional stimulus*, as presented in Table 2.2 and Figure 2.2. **The second terms** are the comparisons or discriminative stimuli. Comparisons include

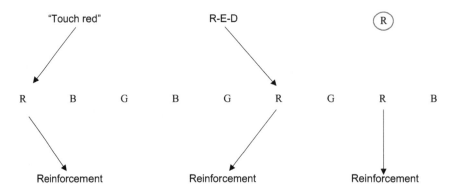

Figure 2.2 Examples of Trials to Train Three Conditional Discriminations (E.g., Matching Colors and Their Spoken Words)

the correct choice, often called the S+, and the incorrect choices, referred to as S- stimuli. Discriminative stimuli are stimuli that are capable of evoking responses because doing so in the past has been followed by reinforcement (e.g., the examples in Table 2.1 and 2.2). **The third term** is the student's response or behavior. **The last term (fourth)** is the consequence (e.g., reinforcement for correct responding or the absence of reinforcement or reprimands for incorrect responses).

When teaching via conditional discriminations, the following sequence is typically followed:

First, the teacher displays the comparisons in front of the student. This can be done on tabletop, in a notebook (in which each page presents a trial), on a computer via a program or PowerPoint. It is important to point out the trials for the session should be set up in advance so that the presentations of samples and comparisons are unsystematic and avoid unintentional bias.

After the comparisons have been displayed the teacher presents the sample. The student is then to select the comparison that "matches" the sample. Please note that "matches" is an arbitrary term as the comparison and the sample to be "matched" may bear no physical resemblance to one another, as during "matching" the color to its spoken name and the other two examples in Figure 2.2. In these cases the physically different items are related to one another through instruction and reinforcement and not because of any physical similarity. If the student selects the correct comparison, represented by the arrow, reinforcement is provided. Then, after a few seconds, the next trial is presented.

Definition of Equivalence

In 2018 Critchfield and colleagues cited a 1926 study by Rexroad in which participants were trained to flex their finger when the color green was displayed and then tested, in the absence of training, if they did so when a printed word stimulus G-R-E-E-N was presented as a probe. The results indicated that the participants that had been trained to the color green emitted the same response (flexing their fingers) to the printed word G-R-E-E-N. These results suggested that a relation between these two items, the color green and the printed word G-R-E-E-N, had developed. This occurred even though:

◆ the color green and the printed word green were physically dissimilar;
◆ this relation (e.g., finger movement in response to the printed word G-R-E-E-N) had never been directly taught;
◆ the relation between the color green and printed word green had not been taught or reinforced, in the experimental setting.

These data seemed to fit the definition of a stimulus class, posited by Keller and Shoenfeld (1950; Chapter 1); that is, items that are followed by the same response, in this case, a finger movement, are members of the same concept or class and may be equivalent to one another. It must be noted that the participants were neurotypical college students so it is quite likely that their prior learning histories contributed to their forming a stimulus class containing the color green to the printed word green. Regardless, the point to be made is that the investigation into concepts, and how they form, has been ongoing for some time.

In 1971 Sidman taught a 17-year-old boy with an intellectual disability to match printed words to their spoken names (he was already able match pictures of those printed words to the same spoken names). Figure 2.3, adapted from Sidman (1971), depicts the experimental arrangement.

The arrows in the figure for steps I, II, III and IV start at the sample and point to the comparison (conditional discrimination or four-term contingencies). They were conditional discriminations, or four-term contingencies, because the selection of a picture or printed word, from an array of comparisons, was conditional upon the presentation of a sample—a spoken name (steps I and II)—a picture (step III), or a printed word (step IV). For example, the conditional item was the sample, the discriminative stimulus was the correct choice (picture or printed word), the behavior was selection of a choice item and the consequence was reinforcement.

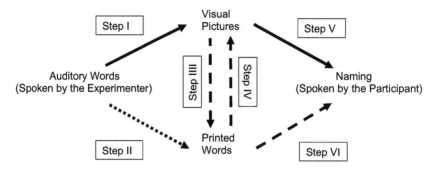

Figure 2.3 The Experimental Arrangement From Sidman, 1971

Steps V and VI were simple discriminations (i.e., naming pictures and printed words, respectively): antecedent = picture or printed word sample; behavior = naming; consequence = reinforcement.

The young man came to the study able to select pictures when their names were spoken (step I) and name those very same pictures (step V). He was then taught to select the printed words, corresponding to the pictures, following their spoken names (step II). Remarkably, following this training, testing revealed that the young man was able to match twenty different pictures to their corresponding printed words (step III), match twenty different printed words to their corresponding pictures (step IV), and name the twenty different printed words (step VI). Sidman labeled these combined performances as *reading comprehension* (relating physically dissimilar visual items, printed words and pictures, to one another, even though the relations between these stimuli had not been directly taught). The participant formed twenty equivalence classes (or concepts), consisting of the spoken word, a picture and a printed word, such that each element became mutually substitutable for the other. Although there were a number of extraordinary outcomes of this ground-breaking study, perhaps the most important, from an instructional point of view, were the formation of twenty distinct classes (concepts) based on reading comprehension and *the emergence of sixty untrained academic skills after teaching only twenty.*

Between 1971 and 1982 there were a number of studies investigating the phenomenon called **stimulus equivalence** but it wasn't until 1982 that the formal properties required for equivalence were identified and defined (Sidman & Tailby, 1982; the reader is directed to this paper for a more detailed discussion of these properties). For a class of stimuli to be considered an equivalence class (concept) the properties of reflexivity, symmetry and transitivity must be satisfied. Before presenting these properties there are certain **conventions** that must be observed. They follow.

First, three concepts, or classes, must be taught at the same time. Thus, if one is teaching colors then three color concepts (e.g., redness, greenness, blueness) must be taught together;

Second, the concept, or class, to be taught, must have a minimum of *three* members, as in the geometry (e.g., rectangle, rhombus, trapezoid) and color (e.g., red, green, blue) examples, in Chapter 1;

Third, N-1 relations between stimuli must be taught, in which N equals the number of potential members in each class (Critchfield & Fienup, 2008). Thus, if one wishes to establish a class of three members ($N = 3$), then two relations between the three members must be taught; if one wishes to establish a class of ten members ($N = 10$), then nine relations between the ten members must be taught;

Fourth, the relations taught must have one stimulus in common. For example, if a class was to contain the items A, B, and C, then two relations must be taught $(N - 1)$ that share one item in common (e.g., A-to-B and A-to-C, in which A is the common element);

Fifth, as a rule, correct responses during training trials are followed by reinforcement whereas responses during test trials, correct or incorrect, are not followed by any consequence. The goal during training is to establish relations between items and to do so one must teach and reinforce the correct responses. However, whether or not the student is capable of reflexivity, symmetry and transitivity is determined by the emergence of these relations during *testing, in the absence of any feedback*. If one were to reinforce responses on test trials then this would no longer be assessing for the emergence of these properties but instead actually teaching them.

Reflexivity

Simply speaking, reflexivity occurs when a student can match items based on physical identity (e.g., matching a comparison to a sample that looks exactly like the sample). Suppose a teacher wants to create a class of items that includes the various representations of the colors (e.g., the colors and their corresponding spoken and printed words). Figure 2.4 presents two examples of how testing may be constructed to test for reflexivity.

Each item serves as the sample and a comparison and the correct choice is a physically identical comparison.

The examples in Figure 2.4 represent test trials and, as such, there is no reinforcement following either correct or incorrect responses, as indicated by the notation "0" (no feedback regardless of the student's selection).

Figure 2.4 Testing Arrangement For Reflexivity

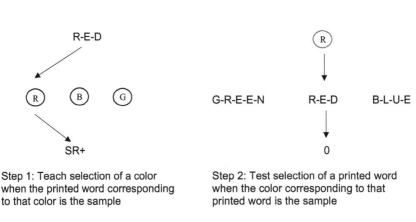

Step 1: Teach selection of a color when the printed word corresponding to that color is the sample

Step 2: Test selection of a printed word when the color corresponding to that printed word is the sample

Figure 2.5 Teaching and Testing Arrangements to Document Symmetry

Symmetry

Symmetry occurs when a student can accurately perform the reverse of a previously taught skill, without being trained to do so. This has been called a sample-comparison reversibility test (Dube et al., 1993). Figure 2.5 illustrates this property. In step 1, the student was taught to select a color (comparisons) when the corresponding printed word appeared as the sample. Step 2 is the test for symmetry as the sample and comparison stimuli are reversed, with printed words serving as comparisons with a color as the sample.

Since step 1 is a teaching trial, correct student answers are reinforced, as designated by the notation, "SR+." Step 2 represents a test trial and, thus, there is no reinforcement following any student answer, as indicated by the notation "0." If the student can reliably perform step two after mastering step 1, then symmetry has been demonstrated.

Transitivity

The third property required to document the formation of equivalence classes is transitivity. Transitivity is said to have occurred when, after teaching two relations in which two items are each related to the *same third* item, testing reveals that all three have become related to one another. This occurs even though not all the relations between the three items were directly taught. As Figure 2.6 shows, a student is first taught to select colors (step 1) and then printed words (step 2), following their spoken names. Then, the student is tested to determine if she can select colors when the corresponding printed word is the sample (step 3) *and* select printed words when a color is the sample (step 4). As previously noted, steps 1 and 2 are training trials, and as such, correct responses are reinforced. Steps 3 and 4 are test trials, and, as such, no reinforcement follows responding.

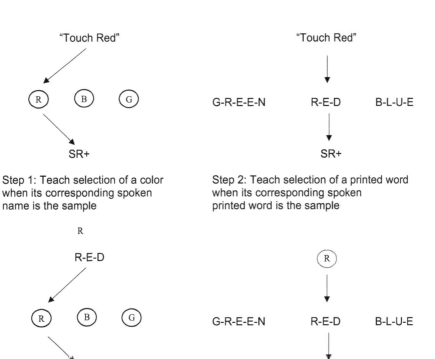

Figure 2.6 Teaching and Testing Arrangement For Transitivity

The use of spoken words (auditory items) as elements make the tests for equivalence difficult to conduct. For example, how does one present auditory items, spoken by the teacher, as *comparisons* to be matched to an identical *sample* (e.g., reflexivity) or a visual sample (e.g., symmetry and transitivity)? It can be done (Dube et al., 1993) but to do so may be beyond the resources of a classroom teacher. Regardless, assuming that the classes to be formed contain no more than one auditory element, then the emergence of all other relations is sufficient to document equivalence class formation, i.e., the combined tests of symmetry and transitivity (Sidman & Tailby, 1982).

Efficiency

A common outcome of EBI is that more and different skills emerge than were directly taught.

Figure 2.7 presents a schematic referred to as the Sidman triangle or the stimulus equivalence triangle (Sidman, 1994). Since $N = 3$ (the number of members in each concept or class) two relations ($N - 1$) between the items in the class must be taught. By convention, solid arrows between stimuli indicate directly taught relations and dashed arrows indicate the relations tested for emergence, in the absence of teaching. Again, the arrows start at the sample and point to the comparison.

Two relations were taught (A-B and A-C), with A serving as the sample and the common element during instruction; the common element is also called a node (Fields et al., 1984). As a result, four relations may emerge, indicated by the dashed lines, without having been directly taught.

Of course, concepts (classes) may contain more than three members, as illustrated in Table 2.2, (adapted from Arntzen, 2012), which illustrates how many relations must be trained and how many relations may emerge, based on the number of potential members in the class. In this example, the number of classes to be trained has been held at three, as this is the minimum for EBI, but, in reality, there is no reason why additional classes could not be taught, other than it gets a bit complicated.

Figure 2.7 Diagram of a Typical Teaching and Testing Sequence to Establish an Equivalence Class (after Sidman, 1971)

Table 2.3 Formula to Determine the Number of Potential Emergent Relations Based on Class Size (after Arntzen, 2012)

Potential Numbers		C x (M-1)	C x (M-1)²
Classes (C)	of Members per Class (M)	Trained Relations	Emergent Relations
3	3	6	12
3	4	9	27
3	5	12	48
3	6	15	75

Note: This analysis excludes identity matching-to-sample trials or reflexivity.

So, to establish three classes of three members each, one must teach six relations (two for each class, $N - 1 = 3 - 1 = 2$, times 3 classes = 6). As a consequence, if instruction is conducted correctly, in addition to the six directly taught skills, another twelve skills emerge, without training, across the three classes. This ratio of taught-to-emergent skills is 1:2 (for every skill taught another two emerge for free; Critchfield & Fienup, 2008). This ratio increases as the number of members within each class increases. For example, if one wishes to teach three classes of four members each then one must teach nine relations (three for each class, $N - 1 = 4 - 1 = 3$, times 3 classes = 9) and, as a result, twenty-seven relations emerge for free. This ratio of taught-to-emergent skills is 1:3 (for every skill taught another three emerge for free). Table 2.3, after Arntzen (2012), details the number of trained and emergent relations based on class size.

Summary

As reported in Chapter 1, EBI has the potential to establish sophisticated and complex concepts with a wide variety of students and individuals. This chapter documented some of the basics associated with teaching to form such classes, such as:

   ◆ Discrete trial training and matching-to-sample;
   ◆ Simple and conditional discriminations;
   ◆ Teaching sequence for conditional discriminations;
   ◆ The definition of equivalence;

- ◆ A review of the seminal study by Sidman (1971);
- ◆ A list of conventions associated with EBI (number of classes, number of members of each class, number of relations to be taught, the necessity of nodes, no feedback during testing);
- ◆ The properties of reflexivity, symmetry and transitivity;
- ◆ The efficiency of EBI.

Recommendations

1   **At a minimum, teach at least two, preferably three, discriminations simultaneously.** The reason for this is that if a single skill is taught, in isolation, it may compete with the acquisition of subsequent, new skills, especially if the new item appears as the incorrect choice in new teachings. For example, a student is taught to select the color red when the teacher says "Touch red," in isolation of other discriminations. Once the student has learned this relation, if the color red appears as an incorrect choice on subsequent teachings (e.g., "Touch green" or "Touch blue") then it may prevent the student from selecting the correct choice on these trials (e.g., green or blue, respectively) because of red's recent history of being the only correct choice; that is, the student may gravitate to the color red, regardless of the direction, because of its recent history of being the only correct choice.

2   **Evaluate the potential reinforcers to be used.** Vocal praise from the teacher is a commonly used consequence in classrooms. However, for a number of students, praise may not function as a reinforcer. Be sure that the consequence one uses during instruction has been documented as a reinforcer (Cooper et al., 2020).

3   **Use an errorless teaching protocol, whenever possible.** Sidman & Stoddard (1967) noted that students who committed errors during instruction tended to fall back on that error pattern whenever the task became difficult (see Chapter 3). Thus, the occurrence of errors may beget future errors.

4   **Do not use a correction procedure.** Correcting errors is akin to "shutting the barn door after the horses are out." Given the plethora of effective and efficient antecedent and errorless teaching procedures, why would one use a trial-and-error method or an error correction procedure? As noted above, errors may increase the likelihood of future errors (Sidman & Stoddard, 1967) and may interfere with the acquisition of new skills (Grow & LeBlanc, 2013).

References

Arntzen, E. (2012). Training and testing parameters in formation of stimulus equivalence: Methodological issues. *European Journal of Behavior Analysis*, *13*, 123–135.

Cooper, J. O., Heron, T. E., & Heward, W. L. (2020). *Applied behavior analysis* (3rd ed.). Pearson.

Critchfield, T. S. (2018). Efficiency is everything: Promoting efficient practice by harnessing derived stimulus relations. *Behavior Analysis in Practice, 11*, 206–210. https://doi.org/10.1007/s40617-018-0262-8

Critchfield, T. S., & Fienup, D. M. (2008). Stimulus equivalence. In S. F. Davis & W. F. Buskist (Eds.), *21st century psychology* (pp. 360–372). Sage.

Dib, N., & Sturmey, P. (2007). Reducing student stereotypy by improving teachers' implementation of discrete-trial teaching. *Journal of Applied Behavior Analysis, 40*(2), 339–343. https://doi.org/10.1901/jaba.2007.52-06

Dube, W. V., Green, G., & Serna, R. W. (1993). Auditory successive conditional discrimination and auditory stimulus equivalence classes. *Journal of the Experimental Analysis of Behavior, 59*(1), 103–114.

Fields, L., Verhave, T., & Fath, S. (1984). Stimulus equivalence and transitive associations: A methodological analysis. *Journal of the Experimental Analysis of Behavior, 42*, 143–157. https://doi.org/10.1901/jeab.1984.42-143

Grow, L., & LeBlanc, L. (2013). Teaching receptive language skills: Recommendations for instructors. *Behavior Analysis in Practice, 6*(1), 56–75. https://doi.org/10.1007/BF03391791

Higbee, T., Aporta, A. P., Resende, A., Nogueira, M., Goyos, C., & Pollard, J. S. (2016). Interactive computer training to teach discrete-trial instruction to undergraduates and special educators in Brazil: A replication and extension. *Journal of Applied Behavior Analysis, 49*, 780–793. https://doi.org/10.1002/jaba.329

Keller, F. S., & Schoenfeld, W. N. (1950). *Principles of psychology*. Appleton-Century-Crofts.

Lerman, D. C., Valentino, A. L., & LeBlanc, L. A. (2016). Discrete trial training. In R. Lang, T. B. Hancock, & N. N. Singh (Eds.), *Early intervention for young children with autism spectrum disorder* (pp. 47–83). Springer International Publishing.

Rexroad, C. N. (1926). Verbalization in multiple choice reactions. *Psychological Review, 33*, 451–458. https://doi.org/10.1037/h0075682

Sidman, M. (1971). Reading and auditory-visual equivalences. *Journal of Speech & Hearing Research, 14*(1), 5–13. https://doi.org/10.1044/jshr.1401.05

Sidman, M. (1994). *Equivalence relations and behavior: A research story*. Authors Cooperative. ISBN-13:978–0962331169

Sidman, M., & Stoddard, L. T. (1967). Effectiveness of fading in programming a simultaneous form discrimination for retarded children. *Journal of the Experimental Analysis of Behavior*, *10*(1), 3–15. https://doi.org/10.1901/jeab.1967.10–3

Sidman, M., & Tailby, W. (1982). Conditional discrimination vs. matching to sample: An expansion of the testing paradigm. *Journal of the Experimental Analysis of Behavior*, *37*(1), 5–22. https://doi.org/10.1901/jeab.1982.37-5

3

Introduction to Sorting

Megan Breault

In a sorting task, one is provided with multiple items that are related to one another in some manner that are to be grouped, based on a rule (see the discussion of concepts in Chapter 1). We use sorting regularly in our everyday lives: sorting plates by size as we take them out of the dishwasher before putting them away, sorting laundry, and when putting away groceries into different sections of the refrigerator. Let's look closer at sorting when doing laundry. In this example, an individual has a hamper full of dirty clothes. They take a white shirt out of the hamper and place it on the floor to the left. The next shirt they take out the hamper is also white; they place this shirt on top of the other white shirt creating the "lights" pile. The next article of clothing is a dark blue shirt, so the sorter creates a new pile for "dark" clothing. Let's imagine that this continues until the individual comes across a towel, which they may want to wash separately. Depending on the individual's laundry washing rules they may sort the towel based on its color or start a new pile for towels. If they come across a sweater next that needs to be washed on delicate, they may create a fourth pile. When the hamper of dirty clothes is empty the sorting task is completed. In this scenario, the number of piles that each person has may be different based on their rules of how they wash their laundry.

Children also naturally encounter sorting activities daily. Let's look at another example of sorting where there is a predetermined number of piles for items to be placed into. When cleaning a playroom after playing with multiple toys, the playroom may have a variety of toys left out that need to be

DOI: 10.4324/9781003297161-3

put into the baskets where they belong. The child picks up a block and puts it in the basket that has other blocks in it. The next toy the child picks up is a toy car, this goes in the basket that has other toy vehicles in it. The third basket may have arts-and-craft items in it, and the child puts the crayons played with into this basket. When all the toys have been placed in their appropriate bins, the child has completed the sorting activity. In this example the items already in the bins signaled where each new toy was to be placed.

Early classification skills such as sorting by items, shapes and colors are developmental milestones demonstrated by typically developing children by the age of two years old. Sorting is also often used in classrooms to teach and assess classification and discrimination skills (Serna et al., 1997). These activities are common in early childhood education curricula, as sorting is a skill important for early language development and other academic skills. Additionally, sorting tests are often used in the field of psychology (Green, 1990) to measure a variety of executive functioning skills.

While less common in behavior analytic research, sorting has begun to receive some attention by those researching equivalence-based instruction. As mentioned in Chapter 2, **match-to-sample** procedures are most often used for teaching and testing in equivalence-based instruction. When working with young children and individuals with developmental disabilities, using matching-to-sample tasks for pretests and posttests can often be lengthy and may be troublesome for some, as reinforcement is not provided during testing (see Chapter 5). Imagine you are going to be conducting a study using equivalence-based instruction with a young learner with the goal to establish three different three-member classes. Figure 3.1 shows an example of the three different three-member classes to potentially be formed after teaching.

However, before teaching to establish classes one needs to determine that the student needs to be taught the skills in question (e.g., that the student does not already possess the skills to be taught; Arntzen & Eilertsen, 2020). To

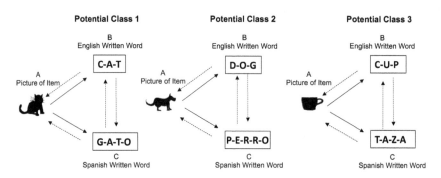

Figure 3.1 Three Potential Three-Member Stimulus Classes to be Formed

do so, one must conduct pretests and this requires at least nine MTS pretests. Using the items depicted in Figure 3.1, the teacher would need to test the student's ability on the following assessments:

> Three different identity matching-to-sample tests (IDMTS), each one assessing the student's ability in matching pictures (cat, dog, and cup), to identical samples of pictures of a cat, dog and cup. Another IDMTS test would assess matching of English-printed words C-A-T, D-O-G, and C-U-P to identical samples of C-A-T, D-O-G, and C-U-P. A third IDMTS test would assess matching of Spanish-printed words G-A-T-O, P-E-R-R-O, and T-A-Z-A to identical samples of G-A-T-O, P-E-R-R-O, and T-A-Z-A.

It is sometimes helpful to represent the teaching targets by alphanumeric notations. In Figure 3.1, the pictures are labeled as "A" items. Thus, the picture of the cat would be labeled A1 (the A notation represents a picture and the numeral 1 represents its potential membership in class 1, Figure 3.1). Applying this logic to other pictures, then dog would be labeled A2 and the cup, A3. Given this approach, and the example in Figure 3.1 then the matching of picture comparisons to identical samples may be represented as A1-A1 (cat-to-cat), A2-A2 (dog-to-dog) and A3 (cup-to-cup). This same alphanumeric method may be applied to the English- and Spanish-printed words as well.

Then, two tests must be conducted to pretest the relations to be trained, in this case, matching English-printed words C-A-T, D-O-G, and C-U-P to their corresponding pictures and matching Spanish-printed words G-A-T-O, P-E-R-R-O, and T-A-Z-A, again, to their corresponding pictures;

Next, the symmetrical relations to the relations to be taught, discussed above, need to be pretested. These include matching pictures to English-printed word samples and matching pictures to Spanish-printed word samples;

Finally, transitive relations would be assessed. Given the sequence presented above, these would include pretesting the student's matching of English-printed words to Spanish-printed words.

As the reader can see, to pretest all the possible relations requires nine pretests (i.e., three IDMTS tests, two tests to assess relations to be trained, two tests to assess symmetrical relations and two tests to assess transitive relations). Additionally, each test must include multiple trials, at least three to six, to assess each individual relation. Finally, testing would also need to be done in the absence of feedback. And, following training, one would also conduct all these tests again as a posttest to document whether or not the student formed the teacher-desired classes. As the reader can see, the development and administration of these tests will require substantial time and effort on the parts of both the teacher and student (Critchfield, 2018). It has also been suggested that conducting the lengthy and labor-intensive pretests and posttests, in the absence of feedback regarding student selections, may lead to challenging behavior or inaccurate student performance (LeBlanc et al., 2003). This has led to modifications for testing procedures that would reduce these risks. Sorting has been suggested as one alternative method that may reduce the duration of such tasks. Rather than conducting the nine pretests, studies that have used sorting tests have presented all the items to the learner and given them the direction to sort them as they want. Figure 3.2 provides two examples of what the outcomes of a sorting test might look like.

If the results of a sorting test matched those of example 1, this would be considered a correct sort, as the learner sorted based on the **experimenter's defined classes**. In this example each item of the stimulus classes 1, 2, and 3

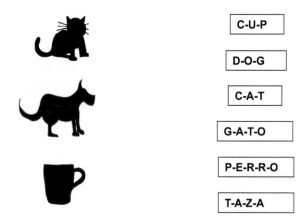

Figure 3.2 Potential Results of a Sorting Test

are sorted together. As will be presented later in this chapter, these results would suggest that these items are now equivalent with one another. If the learner responded as in example 2, this would be considered an incorrect sort. The participant sorted the items based on their own rules and created two piles: one for pictures and one for words. This chapter will examine how sorting can be used as a tool to quickly test if the learner sorted items into experimenter-defined classes or if other critical features are controlling responses.

Sorting in Equivalence Research

In 1992, Cowley, Green and McMorrow conducted one of the first equivalence studies to include sorting tests. The purpose was to teach individuals with traumatic brain injury to relate therapists' faces, printed names and spoken names to one another. Unfortunately, it is common for individuals with traumatic brain injury to have trouble recognizing faces. During sorting tests, the participants were given pictures of therapists' faces, the therapists' handwritten names and the therapists' name plates, with the direction to put the cards that go together into piles. Sorting was scored as correct when all the items of an experimenter-defined group were in a pile with no other items. Pretest outcomes revealed that the participants did not initially sort these items according to experimenter-defined classes. Following training to select the therapists' faces when presented with their names, the participants demonstrated accurate sorting during posttests. Interestingly, the participants sorting scores matched their performance on MTS posttests for emergent equivalence relations. Thus, it appeared that sorting produced the same outcomes as the lengthy and labor-intensive MTS tests (Critchfield, 2018).

These results have been replicated by other studies. In 2011, Arntzen and colleagues used sorting before and after MTS sessions. During initial pretest sorting tasks, none of the participants sorted items into classes accurately. Posttests indicated that nineteen of twenty participants demonstrated accurate sorting. Arntzen et al. (2011) suggested that the presentation of the task in a sorting format may be easier than when presented via match-to-sample since once an item has been sorted to a pile, the item remains there and may serve as a visual prompt to the learner for future items to sort. Fields et al. (2014) also addressed this issue and suggested that when using cards to sort, if cards are stacked on top of one another, it may be possible that only the top card on the pile signals to the learner which item should be sorted there. It was suggested that by conducting multiple sorting tests and shuffling cards each time, the likelihood of false positive test results could be reduced.

In 2012, Fields and colleagues used a sorting task to demonstrate relations between items after being established with match-to-sample procedures. Thirty college students served as participants. All participants were given a sorting task, followed by teaching trials using MTS, presented using a computer software program. The software allowed for data to be collected on reaction time, responses, and duration of tasks. After teaching, all participants were presented with tests for emergent relations using MTS procedures followed by a sorting test. Results of the sorting test across participants closely corresponded to their match-to-sample posttests. Additionally, it was reported that tests for emergent relations performed via match-to-sample procedures took participants thirty minutes compared to the sorting task which took two minutes. These results suggested that sorting tasks may not only be as accurate as MTS test outcomes, but a more time-efficient method to test for emergent class formation.

While the previous studies reviewed included tests of sorting to determine if equivalent relations remained intact when assessed in a novel way, additional studies have since compared the results of sorting tests to the tests for emergent relations via match-to-sample procedures. Simply put, these investigations looked to answer the question, "Could sorting tests be used to show equivalent relations instead of match-to-sample tests?" An important consideration when using sorting is that for relations to be determined emergent, pretest scores would need to show that the participant was not able to sort the items into experimenter-defined classes prior to training. Fields et al. (2014) identified that of fourteen equivalence studies that used sorting tests, only four assessed sorting performances before and after training.

Arntzen et al. (2015) argued that because match-to-sample posttests typically preceded sorting posttests, the results may be viewed as only measuring students' maintenance of emergent relations and not as proof of the emergence of untaught relations. Sixteen typically developing adults participated in the study. Some participants were provided with a sorting test for class formation before they were provided with the MTS tests for emergent relations. Results indicated that the participants were able to sort the items into experimenter-defined classes, and went on to respond correctly for tests conducted via MTS. This was a significant finding, as it was the first study that arranged for testing to occur so that emergent class formation was demonstrated via sorting prior to any tests using MTS procedures. Although one might argue that a sorting test does not allow for reflexivity, symmetry, and transitivity to be demonstrated, Arntzen and colleagues suggested that because participants went on to perform correctly when presented with the MTS tests of reflexivity, symmetry and transitivity, "the classes documented by the outcomes of the sorting tests appear to have the definitional properties of equivalence classes" (2015, p. 623). Regardless, Chapter 9 provides a modified sorting protocol that allows for the assessment of reflexivity, symmetry and transitivity.

In 2020, Arntzen and Eilertsen demonstrated how sorting can be a helpful tool to identify which skills to teach using equivalence-based instruction. Twenty-two university students were taught nutritional information. Participants were first given a sorting task in which they were asked to sort names of food items into one of three carbohydrate values. The sorting results were used to identify which items the participants inaccurately sorted, and training was individualized so that each participant was only taught the values of food items they had incorrectly sorted. By using sorting to assess only the relations that the participant did not know, the experimenters were able to quickly identify what to teach and were able to reduce the amount of time spent teaching. After teaching using an MTS procedure, posttests were conducted using MTS followed by a sorting test. Results showed responding for MTS tests and sorting tests were comparable. Arntzen and Eilertsen suggested that sorting tests could be useful in applied settings, as not only were they time-efficient, but easy to administer.

As previously noted, conducting MTS tests via tabletop requires a great deal of time, planning and effort. For example, those implementing the MTS must counterbalance items across trials (e.g., the unsystematic and unpredictable presentation of different items as samples and comparisons in different positions, in the presence of different samples), deliver appropriate directions, and deliver appropriate consequences (including not providing feedback for responses). Additionally, data must be collected for each trial. By conducting tests via sorting, the effort required by the administrator of the test is significantly reduced across all these areas and data are collected after the participant has completed the sorting task. In fact, it is not unusual for sorting posttests to be documented via a photograph of the final sorting product (Palmer et al., 2021). The decreases in time and effort needed for testing may be an additional benefit of sorting tests in applied settings.

The studies reviewed up to this point have been conducted primarily with typically developing adults. In 2021, Palmer and colleagues used sorting as a test for equivalent relations with three individuals with autism spectrum disorder, aged twelve to twenty-one. A sorting task served as the pretest and following teaching and tests for emergent relations via MTS, a final sorting test was conducted. Results with this population were similar to previous research with adults: participants' performances on MTS tests for equivalence corresponded with their sorting performance. Palmer et al. suggested that "For this population the advantage of sorting as the pre- and post-test measured was that it significantly reduced exposure to tests without reinforcement and reduced the amount of time away from their regularly scheduled school activities" (2021, p. 15).

Research has suggested that sorting tests can be a time-efficient method for conducting pretests and posttests when using equivalence-based instruction. While this testing method is less common than the traditional MTS tests, those using equivalence-based instruction in applied settings may find sorting as an effective alternative as it reduces the amount of time that learners must respond in the absence of reinforcement. Additionally, having tests provided in this format reduces the effort of those delivering instruction, as well as the student taking the tests, and provides a labor-reduced alternative for teachers and students. When presented via tabletop, sorting eliminates multiple trials and therefore reduces the likelihood that there will be errors. If tests are being presented via a computer, sorting may significantly reduce the amount of time spent preparing materials. Equivalence-based instruction's everyday use in classrooms for individuals with developmental disabilities could allow for more time to be devoted to teaching other academic skills. Unfortunately, incorporation of equivalence-based instruction into educational curricula for individuals with autism and other developmental disabilities has been limited (Sidman, 1994). The practicality of sorting tests may allow for those in applied settings to integrate EBI into their everyday teaching methodologies.

Recommendations

1 Sorting tests should be conducted before and after conducting any teaching trials.
2 Determine how many sorting tests are to be conducted. It is recommended that multiple sorting tests, assessing the same relations, be conducted to verify the reliability of the findings.
3 Determine how many sorting trials will make up a sorting test. Arntzen et al. (2015) suggested that having multiple sorting trials could rule out the potential of false positive responses.
4 Decide how you will present sorting tasks. In some sorting tests the experimenters have asked participants to sort the materials into a set number of piles. Others have provided participants with cards that served as signals of the piles to be sorted into, or have asked participants to group them however they see fit. By allowing the participant to sort as they want, one may assess if there are any preexisting rules that the learner may have about the items being sorted. On the

other hand, by providing a card to be matched to may allow for the specific assessments of different types of relations (e.g., reflexivity, symmetry and transitivity; see Chapter 9).

5   Similar to MTS tests, pretests and posttests that use sorting should be conducted in the absence of any feedback.

How to Use Sorting via Tabletop Methods

1   Identify the potential stimulus classes that you would like to be formed.
2   Make cards for each of the items in your stimulus class. Make sure that these cards are all the same size.
3   Shuffle cards and put them in a pile.
4   Give the cards to the learner and say, "Put these cards into piles that go together."
    Note: See Chapter 9 for a detailed outline regarding how to use sorting to assess specifically for reflexivity, symmetry and transitivity, as the sorting protocol for each is different.
5   When the cards have been sorted into piles, take a picture of the final product. Do not provide any feedback to the learner on their response during or after the sorting task.

Record the number of correct items in each pile. Record how many items were in the wrong pile. Missing cards belonging to a pile that were sorted into other piles should be scored as minuses. Divide the number of correct items sorted by the total number of items and multiply by 100 to get the percentage of correct items sorted.

Table 3.1 may prove helpful, using the following example. Assume that the sorting task is arranged in such a manner that a different card is placed

Table 3.1 Scoring Student Grouping of Comparisons Via Sorting

		Comparisons		
		B1	**B2**	**B3**
Samples	A1			
	A2			
	A3			

face up in front of each of the three boxes, to serve as a sample (e.g., A1, A2, and A3). Also assume that the student is then given a stack of eighteen randomly shuffled cards, representing other teaching targets B1, B2, and B3 (six of each). The student is then to place in boxes those B teaching targets that go with the A items. The teacher can score a slash mark in the cell that intersects the specific B comparison placed in an A sample box.

6   Teach the learner the required conditional discriminations using match-to-sample procedures (see Chapter 2).
7   When the learner has met mastery criteria for the relations to be trained, complete the sorting task again, as a posttest (repeat steps 3 through 6).
8   If on the final sorting task, the learner sorts the items into experimenter-defined classes, then it may be argued that equivalence has been demonstrated.
9   If the participant does not sort accurately during the initial posttest, then do not provide any feedback and have the participant complete the task again (up to two additional times) to see if the emergence is delayed.

References

Arntzen, E., Braaten, L. F., Lian, T., & Eilifsen, C. (2011). Response-to-sample requirements in conditional discrimination procedures. *European Journal of Behavior Analysis*, 12, 505–522. https://doi.org/10.1080/15021149.2011.11434398

Arntzen, E., & Eilertsen, J. M. (2020). Using stimulus-equivalence technology to teach skills about nutritional content. *Perspectives on Behavior Science*, 43(3), 469–485. https://doi.org/10.1007/s40614-020-00250-2

Arntzen, E., Norbom, A., & Fields, L. (2015). Sorting: An alternative measure of class formation. *Psychological Record*, 65, 615–623. https://doi.org/10.1007/S40732-015-0132-5

Cowley, B. J., Green, G., & Braunling-McMorrow, D. (1992). Using stimulus equivalence procedures to teach name-face matching to adults with brain injuries. *Journal of Applied Behavior Analysis*, 25, 461–475. https://doi.org/10.1901/jaba.1992.25-461

Critchfield, T. S. (2018). Efficiency is everything: Promoting efficient practice by harnessing derived stimulus relations. *Behavior Analysis in Practice*, 11, 206–210. https://doi.org/10.1007/s40617-018-0262-8

Fields, L., Arntzen, E., & Moksness, M. (2014). Stimulus sorting: A quick and sensitive index of equivalence class formation. *The Psychological Record*, *64*, 487–498. https://doi.org/10.1007/s40732–014–0034-y

Fields, L., Arntzen, E., Nartey, R. K., & Eilifsen, C. (2012). Effects of a meaningful, a discriminative and a meaningless stimulus on equivalence class formation. *Journal of the Experimental Analysis of Behavior, 97*(2), 163–181. https://doi.org/10.1901/jeab.2012.97-163

Green, G. (1990). Differences in development of visual and auditory-visual equivalence classes, natural categories and cross-modal perception. *American Journal on Mental Retardation, 95*, 260–270.

LeBlanc, L. A., Miguel, C. F., Cummings, A. R., Goldsmith, T. R., & Car, J. E. (2003). The effects of three stimulus-equivalence teaching conditions on emergent US geography relations of children diagnosed with ASD. *Behavioral Interventions, 18*, 279–283. https://doi.org/10.1002/bin.144

Palmer, S. K., Maguire, R. W., Lionello-DeNolf, K. M., & Braga-Kenyon, P. (2021). Expansion of Sidman's theory: The inclusion of prompt stimuli in equivalence classes. *Journal of the Experimental Analysis of Behavior, 115*(1), 255–271. https://doi.org/10.1002/JEAB.655

Serna, R. W., Dube, W. V., & Mcllvane, W. J. (1997). Assessing same/different judgments in individuals with severe intellectual disabilities: A status report. *Research in Developmental Disabilities, 18*, 343–368.

Sidman, M. (1994). *Equivalence relations and behavior: A research story*. Authors Cooperative.

4

Teaching and Testing for Classes
Russell W. Maguire and Ronald F. Allen

Overview

Remember, equivalence-based instruction *requires* that *at least* three potential classes of *at least* three members, each, be taught together. To illustrate, let's assume that a teacher wishes to teach a student, whose heritage language is Spanish, to relate the English and Spanish words for animals. To do so, the teacher plans to establish three different classes (class 1, class 2 and class 3), each consisting of three items (A, B and C). Class 1 is the dog class, class 2 is the cow class and class 3 is the pig class. The A items represent the Spanish printed words for dog, cow and pig, the B items represent pictures of the dog, cow and pig, and the C items represent the English printed words for dog, cow and pig. Figure 4.1 presents the different items according to their potential class membership.

Thus
- The A1, A2 and A3 items correspond to the Spanish printed words P-E-R-R-O, V-A-C-A and C-E-R-D-O, respectively. The letter indicates the type of item it is (e.g., Spanish-printed word versus English-printed word versus picture) and the numerals indicate class membership (e.g., 1, 2 or 3);
- Similarly, B1, B2 and B3 correspond to the pictures dog, cow and pig, respectively, for classes 1, 2 and 3, respectively;

DOI: 10.4324/9781003297161-4

Classes	"A" Items	"B" Items	"C" Items
1	P-E-R-R-O		D-O-G
2	V-A-C-A		C-O-W
3	C-E-R-D-O		P-I-G

Figure 4.1 Examples of Potential Classes

◆ And C1, C2 and C3 correspond to the English-printed words DOG, COW AND PIG, respectively, for classes 1, 2 and 3, respectively.

A typical sequence of events for an EBI training and testing arrangement, via discrete trial training, may require an excessive number of testing and teaching trials that have the potential to overwhelm the learner, if not the teacher. For this reason, it is recommended that pretests and posttests be conducted via sorting, as described in Chapters 3 and 9.

Pretesting

The purpose of pretesting is to establish that there is a need for instruction. Many students with developmental disabilities require sophisticated instruction across a variety of areas. The last thing one wants to do is waste time on teaching things to a student that she/he/they already know. Figure 4.2 presents the relations that need to be pretested. These are indicated by the bidirectional arrows linking the items. For example, the bidirectional arrow between the Spanish printed word and the picture of the dog means that some trials P-E-R-R-O (A1) is the sample and the picture of the dog (B1) is the comparison and on other trials the bidirectional relation B-A (the picture of the dog (B1) is the sample and the Spanish printed word, P-E-R-R-O (A1) is the comparison).

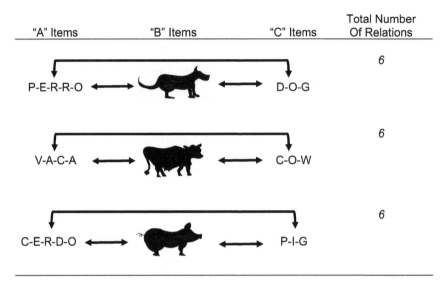

"A" Items	"B" Items	"C" Items	Total Number Of Relations
P-E-R-R-O		D-O-G	6
V-A-C-A		C-O-W	6
C-E-R-D-O		P-I-G	6

Figure 4.2 Number of Relations Between Members Within the Same Class

If using a matching-to-sample format, pretesting would require the assessment of six different relations within each potential class, for a total of 18 relations (Figure 4.1). When one considers that each relation must be assessed on multiple trials, this could easily require 100 or more trials of just pretesting. Also, there is no feedback during testing. Providing feedback during testing is actually teaching and may confound the results (i.e., the learner actually learns the relation between items during testing) or is just accurate enough, due to the presence of reinforcement, to confuse such a determination. To make things easy, a sorting sequence is recommended. Figure 4.3 presents a diagram of a sorting procedure.

The upper portion of Figure 4.3 presents three boxes and the bottom portion represents a pile of randomly shuffled cards, consisting of multiple instances of each item intended to form a class. A sample card is placed in front of each box to which the shuffled comparison cards are "matched" (placed in the box). The sample cards and the comparison cards change depending on the test being conducted (M. Breault, personal communication, January 5, 2022).

It is important to point out that the sorting sequence that follows deviates from the typical one reported in the literature. For example, it is common that participants are given a pile of randomly shuffled cards and instructed to group them as they see fit (i.e., without a sample card in front of each box). The reader can immediately discern that while this procedure documents whether or not the participant can "group" items together, it fails to formally document reflexivity, symmetry and transitivity (Arntzen et al., 2015).

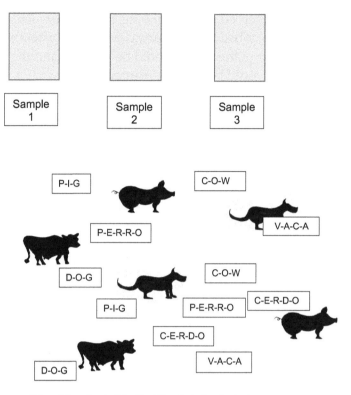

Pile of Randomly Shuffled Cards to be Sorted

Figure 4.3 Examples of a Sorting Pretest and Posttest

To address this shortcoming the sorting procedure presented here has been modified and broken down into multiple, and different, pretests, with a sample card placed in front of each grouping box in an effort to document the critical-features class formation.

To test for **reflexivity**, the comparison cards would consist of items that were identical to one of the three samples (e.g., pictures to identical pictures, printed words to identical printed words, etc.);

- ◆ To test for the **To-Be-Taught** relations, the comparison cards would consist of items used during teaching, to be related to one of the three samples used during teaching. If one was to be taught to select pictures when the samples were English-printed words, then the cards placed in front of the boxes would be English-printed words and the cards to sort into the boxes would be pictures;
- ◆ To test for **Symmetry** the comparison cards would consist of items that served as samples during instruction and the samples would be

the three items that served as comparisons during instruction. Using the example just described above, during symmetry assessments the cards placed in front of the boxes would be pictures and the cards to sort into the boxes would be English-printed words;

- To test for transitivity, the comparison and sample cards would consist of the items that had not been directly related to one another during instruction. For example, if one was to conduct two trainings in which a student was to select pictures when Spanish printed words were the samples and then select pictures when English printed words were the samples (middle panel of Figure 4.4) then transitivity would assess the relations between items that had not been taught: sorting English printed words when Spanish printed words were the sample cards in front of the boxes and sorting Spanish printed words when English printed words were the sample cards in front of the boxes.

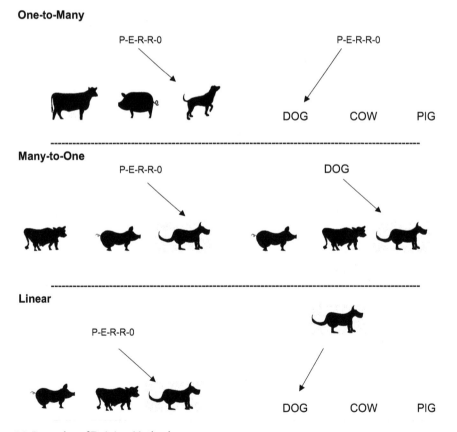

Figure 4.4 Examples of Training Methods

Regardless, during sorting, the student is instructed to place the comparison cards into the boxes, according to how she/he/they think they should be grouped.

Once completed, the teacher can then take a photograph of the finished groupings (a permanent product, Cooper et al., 2020), documenting whether or not the student grouped the items into classes consistent with the teacher's intent. It is recommended that the pretest/posttest sorting be conducted a number of times unless consistent outcomes are obtained.

As previously noted, because the student receives no feedback as to the "correctness" of his/her response during testing, the results of the test may be compromised (e.g., the student may stop responding all together or responding may come under the control of irrelevant features). To remedy this problem, the teacher may reinforce other student behaviors during the sorting process (e.g., attending, on-task, sitting, etc.).

Also, the teacher must decide on an accuracy criterion to determine when a sorting test has demonstrated that the student truly "knows" which items relate to one another. Staying with our dog-cow-pig examples, assume that the sorting pretest required the student to "group" six cards for each item (total = 18). This means that each potential class is represented by six English printed words, six Spanish printed words and six pictures for a total of 18 cards per class. To make a determination that the student has formed a class consisting of the three different items (e.g., an English printed word, a Spanish printed word and a picture) the student should make no more than three incorrect "sorts" per class, *and* no more than one error for each of the different items: an English printed word, a Spanish printed word, and a picture, per class.

Sorting tests might require multiple applications in order for the student to demonstrate consistent groupings.

Teaching

Assuming that the pretest sorting results demonstrate *inaccurate* class formation, it is time to teach. It wasn't until the mid 1980s that the idea of *how* the initial skills were trained was a critical factor as to whether or not equivalence classes would emerge. Saunders and Green (1999) presented perhaps the premier analysis evaluating the three most common methods of training the prerequisite skills: *one-to-many training, linear training and many-to-one training*. According to Saunders and Green (1999), in order for equivalence classes to form, the training of the initial skills must present each item to be taught against each other item to be taught so that the student can discriminate one from another. This can be accomplished within each trial when the comparisons may be discriminated from each other and from the sample. This can also be accomplished across trials when the different sample items are discriminated from each other. Unfortunately, not all the training methods accomplish this goal.

There are three, standard teaching methods. They are one-to-many, many-to-one and linear. In the *one-to-many training* method, *many* comparisons, in this case B and C, are trained to *one* sample (topmost example, Figure 4.4). In the *many-to-one training method,* a comparison is trained to *many* different samples (middle example, Figure 4.4). Finally, in the *linear method,* the comparison from the initial training then appears as the sample during the next training (bottommost example, Figure 4.4).

Research has documented that the Linear training method is the least effective and that the Many-to-One Method is the best of the three (Fields et al., 2020). However, there is some question as to whether or not the One-to-many method may be as effective as the Many-to-one method (Ayres-Pereira & Arntzen, 2019).

It is recommended that teachers use the Many-to-one training method or the One-to-Many training method and not the Linear method. This is particularly important when teaching children or individuals with developmental disabilities as these individuals may lack the necessary skills (e.g., a sophisticated verbal repertoire or wide exposure to a variety of teaching protocols) to overcome the deficits inherent in this training method.

Figures 4.5 and 4.6 present many-to-one training data sheets using the picture of animals and Spanish and English printed words. Figure 4.5 is to teach the student to select a picture when the Spanish printed word appears as the sample and Figure 4.6 is to teach the student to select a picture when the English printed word appears as the sample. Note that as this is a many-to-one teaching method, the "one comparison" is a picture and the many samples are the Spanish and English printed words.

In a typical teaching session, the following sequence of events occur, in order (note: this assumes that the teacher has the instructional setting already set up, including the data sheet (Figure 4.5 and 4.6) and any items to be used to reinforce).

First, the comparisons for a specific trial are displayed, on the tabletop or on a page in a notebook or on the computer;

Second, the sample is displayed, above the comparisons, often accompanied by the teacher's direction to the student to "match";

Trial	Sample Printed Words		Comparisons (Pictures)		
			Left	Middle	Right
1	P-E-R-R-O		Pig	Cow	Dog
2	V-A-C-A		Dog	Cow	Pig
3	C-E-R-D-O		Pig	Dog	Cow
4	V-A-C-A		Pig	Cow	Dog
5	P-E-R-R-O		Cow	Pig	Dog
6	V-A-C-A		Cow	Dog	Pig
7	C-E-R-D-O		Dog	Pig	Cow
8	V-A-C-A		Cow	Pig	Dog
9	C-E-R-D-O		Dog	Cow	Pig
10	P-E-R-R-O		Cow	Dog	Pig
11	V-A-C-A		Pig	Dog	Cow
12	P-E-R-R-O		Dog	Cow	Pig
13	C-E-R-D-O		Cow	Dog	Pig
14	P-E-R-R-O		Dog	Pig	Cow
15	C-E-R-D-O		Cow	Pig	Dog
16	V-A-C-A		Dog	Pig	Cow
17	P-E-R-R-O		Pig	Dog	Cow
18	C-E-R-D-O		Pig	Cow	Dog

Figure 4.5 Sample Data Sheet for Matching Picture Comparisons to Spanish Printed Word Samples

Third, the student responds. During this step a prompt may be employed (see Chapter 5 for a discussion of teaching strategies);

Fourth, correct responses are reinforced and incorrect responses are followed by whatever consequence the teacher is using (see Chapters 5 and 6 for discussions of different consequences that may be used);

Fifth, the items are removed and the teacher scores the student's response. If using the data sheets in Figures 4.5 and 4.6, this can be accomplished by merely circling the item the student selected;

Sixth, the next trial is presented.

Figure 4.7 provides a diagram of steps 1–4.

Conducting Posttests

Let's assume that the teacher decided to use the Many-to-One method of training: teaching the student to select pictures of dogs, cows and pigs, when the samples are first English printed words and then when the samples are Spanish printed words. Once the student has learned these relations, posttest

Trial	Sample Printed Words		Comparisons (Pictures)		
			Left	Middle	Right
1	D-O-G		Pig	Cow	Dog
2	C-O-W		Dog	Cow	Pig
3	P-I-G		Pig	Dog	Cow
4	C-O-W		Pig	Cow	Dog
5	D-O-G		Cow	Pig	Dog
6	C-O-W		Cow	Dog	Pig
7	P-I-G		Dog	Pig	Cow
8	C-O-W		Cow	Pig	Dog
9	P-I-G		Dog	Cow	Pig
10	D-O-G		Cow	Dog	Pig
11	C-O-W		Pig	Dog	Cow
12	D-O-G		Dog	Cow	Pig
13	P-I-G		Cow	Dog	Pig
14	D-O-G		Dog	Pig	Cow
15	P-I-G		Cow	Pig	Dog
16	C-O-W		Dog	Pig	Cow
17	D-O-G		Pig	Dog	Cow
18	P-I-G		Pig	Cow	Dog

Figure 4.6 Sample Data Sheet for Matching Picture Comparisons to English Printed Word Samples

sorting should occur, similar to the pretest sorting, described above. The posttest sorting should be administered on multiple occasions until the student either demonstrates class formation (relates all the items within a class to one another) or his/her/their responses are consistent, although perhaps inaccurate, from the teacher's perspective.

Delayed Emergence

Typically, if done correctly, the untaught relations between items emerge immediately following teaching. However, there are occasions in which such emergence is delayed. Delayed emergence is the phenomenon of the relevant untrained relations or associations between items emerging slowly, over successive test sessions. Although delayed emergence has been widely studied, the reasons for why this occurs are still unclear (Holth & Arntzen, 1998). Sidman (1994) suggested that the formation of equivalence classes may occur slowly as other options drop out and then the learner sorts the relevant items together.

Step	Diagram
1 Display Comparisons	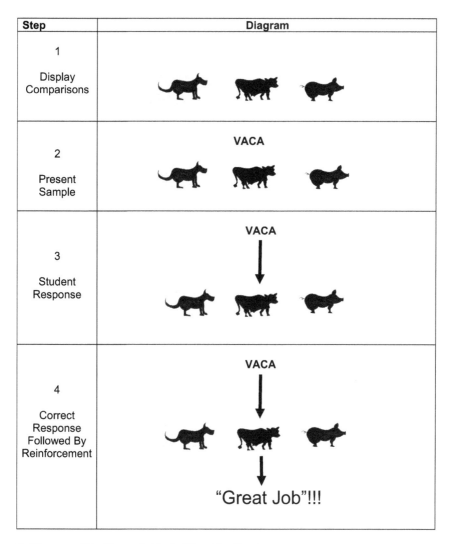
2 Present Sample	
3 Student Response	
4 Correct Response Followed By Reinforcement	

Figure 4.7 Diagram of the Steps of a Typical Teaching Session

When delayed emergence is observed there are a number of options available to the teacher to resolve this situation:

1 If two or three additional posttests does not result in emergence, conduct a refresher training session. It is best if the two relations trained are presented intermixed within the same session, alternating, trial-by-trial, unsystematically. Then test for emergence again.

2 The absence of reinforcement during testing may account for the failure of the untaught relations to emerge. In these cases, it may prove helpful to conduct sorting with some training trials inter-

mixed among the test trials, with reinforcement provided for some, but not all the training trials.

Recommendations

1 Use sorting instead of matching-to-sample for the pretests and posttests. They are quicker and easier, for both the student and the teacher. Chapter 9 provides a detailed description of sorting;
2 Take a photograph of the outcomes of sorting pretests and posttests as data collection. These data can then be transferred to a data sheet documenting class formation, or the lack of formation;
3 Use the many-to-one training method to teach the initial relation between items. Data sheets are presented in Figure 4.4 and 4.5 that a teacher can substitute with their own items.

References

Arntzen, E., Norbom, A., & Fields, L. (2015). Sorting: An alternative measure of class formation. *Psychological Record*, *65*, 615–623. https://doi.org/10.1007/S40732-015-0132-5

Ayres-Pereira, V., & Arntzen, E. (2019). Effect of presenting baseline probes during or after emergent relations tests on equivalence class formation. *The Psychological Record*, *69*, 193–204. https://doi.org/10.1007/s40732-018-0326-8

Cooper, J. O., Heron, T. E., & Heward, W. L. (2020). *Applied behavior analysis* (3rd ed.). Pearson Education.

Fields, L., Arntzen, E., & Doran, E. (2020). Yield as an essential measure of equivalence class formation, other measures and new determinants. *The Psychological Record*, *70*, 175–186. https://doi.org/10.1007/s40732-020-00377-3

Holth, P., & Arntzen, E. (1998). Stimulus familiarity and the delayed emergence of stimulus equivalence or consistent nonequivalence. *The Psychological Record*, *48*(1), 81–110.

Saunders, R. R., & Green, G. (1999). A discrimination analysis of training-structure effects on stimulus equivalence outcomes. *Journal of the Experimental Analysis of Behavior*, *72*, 117–137. https://doi.org/10.1901/jeab.1999.72-117

Sidman, M. (1994). *Equivalence relations and behavior: A research story*. Authors Cooperative. ISBN-13:978-0962331169

5

Teaching Considerations

Multiple-Element Items and Errorless Instruction

Simone Palmer

A primary advantage of equivalence-based instruction is that more untrained academic relations emerge than those that were directly taught. Building on this concept of efficient instruction, this chapter will present additional ways to make equivalence-based instruction more efficacious.

As Sidman (1971) and other researchers have shown, equivalence-based instruction may be used to teach reading comprehension (e.g., establishing relations between printed words and their corresponding pictures and spoken words; see Chapters 1 and 2). Figure 5.1 presents an example of the teaching and training to establish reading comprehension.

Steps 1 and 2 are instructional phases: selecting the picture, based on its spoken name (Step 1, solid line) and then selecting the printed word, again based on its spoken name (Step 2, solid line). Reading comprehension is demonstrated if the learner can then, as a result of this teaching, relate the printed word to its picture (Step 3, dashed line) and the picture to its printed word (Step 4, dashed line), all in the absence of additional training. Although not shown in Figure 5.1, the learner may also be able to accurately name the symbol and the printed word, again, without additional training. Consequently, after teaching two academic skills, four untaught skills may emerge.

What if this efficient method to establish concepts (i.e., classes) could be made even more so? Figure 5.2 presents an alternative. The upper

DOI: 10.4324/9781003297161-5

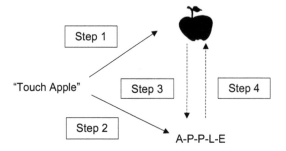

Figure 5.1 Teaching and Testing Arrangement to Establish Reading Comprehension

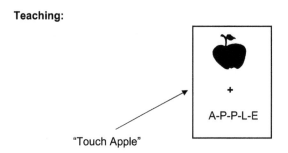

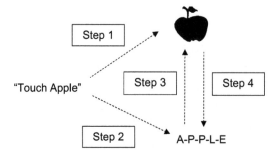

Figure 5.2 Teaching and Testing Arrangement to Establish Reading Comprehension With A Complex Comparison

portion of this figure represents teaching (selecting) a multiple-element item in response to the instructor's spoken direction. Please note that in this arrangement the comparison consists of two elements: a picture and a printed word (the plus symbol [+] is not part of the actual comparison but merely to illustrate that this comparison is a multielement item and two elements appear together).

Testing for emergent relations appears in the lower portion of Figure 5.2. The result of teaching (Step 1) may very well be that the two visual items, the picture and the printed word, not only become related to their spoken word (Steps 1 and 2) but may become related to one another (Steps 3 and 4). Consequently, teaching a single relation involving a two-element comparison may result in one trained relation and the emergence of four untaught relations, making learning even more effective.

As previously noted, to increase the efficiency of instruction, educational programs may use items comprised of multiple elements (Groskreutz et al., 2010; Lovaas et al., 1971; Rosales et al., 2014; Stromer et al., 1993; Yorlets et al., 2018). When items consist of multiple individual elements, they have been referred to as either compound or complex stimuli (Stromer et al., 1993; Yorlets et al., 2018). A compound stimulus is one that consists of multiple, individual elements, and all elements must be present, in a specific order, to occasion correct responding. For example, the printed word C-A-T may be considered a compound stimulus as all the letters are required, in a specific sequence, for one to read or name the compound stimulus "CAT."

On the other hand, a complex stimulus is one that is also comprised of multiple elements, but each individual element, when presented alone, is sufficient to occasion learner responding, similar to that exerted by the multielement item itself. Using the printed-word C-A-T example, presented above, if the instructor's direction was changed from "Touch C-A-T" to "Touch the word that has a 'C'" or "Touch the word that has an 'A,'" then any variation containing the named letter would lead to the correct response.

Many of the stimuli in the natural environment may be considered compound or complex stimuli. For example, words are comprised of a combination of letters and to successfully read those words, one needs to orient to (i.e., pay attention) to all of the letters, in the order provided (i.e., a compound stimulus). Additionally, adjective-noun combinations, multiple digit numerals, mathematical equations, communication modalities including pictures and words, and others may be referred to as compound or complex stimuli.

Using compound or complex stimuli during instruction has been shown to enhance instruction (Groskreutz et al., 2010; Maguire et al., 1994; Yorlets et al., 2018). By including multiple-element items (e.g., presenting a picture and saying its name along with an array of printed words), learners may acquire all of the elements (e.g., spoken words, printed words, and pictures or symbols) simultaneously (Groskreutz et al., 2010). Thus, instead of teaching two or three separate discriminations, using multiple-element teaching targets may result in the acquisition of a number of discriminations as the individual elements become related to one another. Perhaps the most well-known use of

multiple-element items during instruction is the Picture Exchange Communication System (Bondy & Frost, 1998). This is a method of communication
used with nonvocal individuals and presents a printed word simultaneously
with a two-dimensional symbol of a noun or verb, with the goal of both elements eventually controlling communication (e.g., naming or requesting). In
another example, Maguire et al. (1994) used complex samples containing two
and three elements with adults with and without an autism spectrum disorder diagnosis. After teaching with complex items, testing revealed that participants matched the individual elements to the correct comparison, and one
another, without additional training, indicating that these relations between
the individual elements emerged without further instruction. Yorlets et al.
(2018) conducted a study including a complex sample consisting of sign language (ASL) and spoken word to which pictures and printed words were to
be matched to identify different US states. The results indicated the establish-
ment of classes of equivalent items.

As noted above, using multiple-element items during teaching has been
shown to increase the efficiency of instruction. However, the failure to attend
and respond to all the critical aspects of a multiple-element target may interfere with the acquisition of academic and communication skills (e.g., control
by one or some elements and not others; Dube, 2009; Yorlets et al., 2018). This
has been referred to as stimulus overselectivity or restricted stimulus control
(Lovaas et al., 1971; Litrownik et al., 1978; Stromer & Stromer, 1990a, 1990b;
Stromer et al., 1993; Yorlets et al., 2018). For example, if a learner pays attention to *only* the beginning of a word instead of all of the letters presented,
errors in discriminating words that begins with the same initial letter(s) may
occur (e.g., B-A-T versus B-A-G, versus B-A-D, etc.). Stimulus overselectivity was identified over 50 years ago as one of the learning problems for individuals diagnosed with autism spectrum disorder (Lovaas et al., 1971) and
it is still an area of concern for special education professionals. Thus, the
instructor who uses compound or complex items during instruction has the
added responsibility to ensure that the learner attends to *ALL* the relevant
elements.

Overselectivity could explain prompt dependency for some individuals.
A prompt is a supplemental stimulus, added to the instructional arrangement,
that increases the probability of the learner selecting the correct response
(Cooper et al., 2020; MacDuff et al., 2001). Initially, a prompt is added to the
correct answer to establish correct responding and over time the prompt is
faded out. For instance, a teacher may use a point prompt to signal to the
student the correct answer and then, over subsequent trials, gradually fade
out the point prompt with the goal of the correct answer being sufficient to

evoke student responding (Green, 2001; MacDuff et al., 2001; Touchette, 1971; Touchette & Howard, 1984). However, it is not unusual for some students to respond *only* to the prompt and if this occurs the student is unable to respond to the teaching target. This means that the student's correct responding is dependent on the prompt, hence the term prompt dependency. Given that students with developmental disabilities often require prompting during instruction it is imperative that the potential of overselectivity and prompt dependency be planned for and addressed (Hume et al., 2009; MacDuff et al., 2001; Dube & Wilkinson, 2014).

There are several methods to increase the probability that the learner attends to all the relevant elements of a multi-element instructional item and refrains from coming under the restrictive control of isolated elements or prompts. First, prior to each trial the teacher may require the student emit an observing response to each individual element of a multielement item before responding. An observing response is student behavior that indicates to the teacher that the student has seen and attended to the individual elements of the teaching target. This observing response may be non-differential or differential (Dube & Wilkinson, 2014). A non-differential observing response is one that is generic and not unique to the elements attended, such as touching the picture of an apple and then touching the printed word A-P-P-L-E. A differential observing response is one that is specific to each of the elements of a multielement item, such as naming the picture of an apple "apple" and then naming each of the specific letters, in sequence, in the printed word A-P-P-L-E. Of course, observing responses do not guarantee that the student has attended to each item, even if they touch each one, and students may not know the names of each element.

Second, prior to each teaching session students could be exposed to identity-matching to complex samples. For example, a task could be arranged in which a complex teaching target consisting of a picture and a printed word of an apple (Figure 5.2) served as a sample and the comparisons could be individual elements of which only one was part of the sample (i.e., the correct choice). The individual elements of the complex teaching target serve as the correct choice on trials alternating unpredictably (Maguire et al., 1995). If the student was capable of performing this task, then one might assume that he/she has attended to both elements.

Third, alternating the position or placement of the individual elements within the complex teaching target across trials may also increase how much the student attends to each element.

Regardless of the strategy used to improve student attention, if a teacher employs compound or complex stimuli in EIBI, one must take care to design instruction that promotes such attention.

Errorless Instruction

For some learners, instructor directions or the presentation of the instructional items alone may not result in the learner engaging in the desired behavior and their responses may even come under the control of factors beyond what the instructor had planned. Consider a learner who is to select a letter (e.g., A, B or C) after the teacher presents the instruction to touch one of them (e.g., "Touch ___"). For the sake of this discussion, let's assume that the learner always selects the item in the middle of a three-choice array. Under these circumstances, the teacher's direction is not controlling the learner's behavior but rather, the learner's attention and responding are under the control of something only incidental to the instructional arrangement (e.g., position). Worse yet, the learner may continue this behavior because it is intermittently correct, as the correct answer appears in the middle of the array, thereby strengthening the position selection.

Additionally, learners with developmental or learning disabilities *may* need frequent and immediate feedback on their performance and require instructional strategies to avoid or reduce errors (Etzel & LeBlanc, 1979; Lancioni & Smeets, 1986; MacDuff et al., 2001; Sidman & Stoddard, 1966; Farber et al., 2016). Unfortunately, the primary method of instruction for individuals with developmental disabilities may be described as trial-and-error (e.g., differential reinforcement of correct responses; O'Neill et al., 2018). With this method, correct responses are reinforced and incorrect responses go unreinforced. Over trials, the learner "figures out" the correct and incorrect answers. As the reader can see, this is not a very efficient way to teach, especially for individuals with learning challenges. For example, Green (2001) indicated not only may trial-and-error instruction be ineffective, but also have the potential to evoke challenging behavior and avoidance by the learner of the instruction session. More to the point, if one teaches the initial relations to establish equivalence classes poorly, then this may interfere with the emergence of untaught relations and the formation of such classes. For example, Maguire et al., (1988) and Maguire et al., (2018) compared the formation of equivalence classes following trial-and-error training and errorless instruction and the results indicated the superiority of the errorless protocol.

Teaching while minimizing errors has been referred to as errorless learning (or instruction) as discussed above. Lancioni and Smeets (1986) defined errorless instruction as "training with error rates lower than 10% of the responses . . . the initial responding is easy . . . [and] progress toward the final discrimination is gradual" (p. 136). Consider a lesson in identifying letters. The instructor may highlight the correct response (e.g., prompt) with a color initially to show the learner the correct answer, then gradually and systematically fade the highlighting, based on continued correct responding, until the learner can identify the letter in the absence of the color prompt and without errors. Terrace (1963a) and (1963b) suggested that the occurrence of errors during instruction make interfere with and actually prevent the acquisition of the academic skills being taught.

The process of systematically and gradually eliminating prompts is called prompt fading. Prompt-fading procedures can be conducted in a variety of ways. Figure 5.3 provides examples of fading stimulus prompts that may be used during errorless instruction.

The upper left of Figure 5.3 shows a within stimulus prompt (i.e., it is called *within* because a critical feature *within* the training item, in this case, the shape of the letter "M", is exaggerated and cues the learner to the correct answer). Over consecutive correct responses this exaggeration is faded (i.e., made less pronounced) until it is indistinguishable from the other letters.

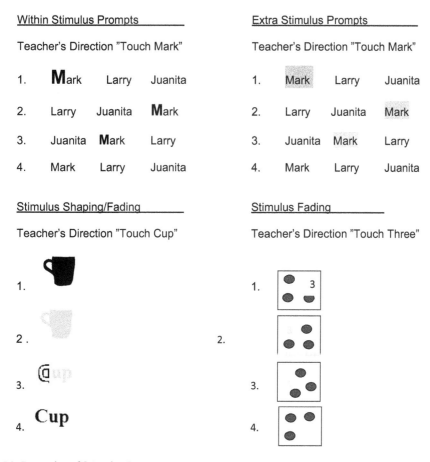

Figure 5.3 Examples of Stimulus Prompts

However, should errors occur the teacher can always introduce additional fading steps, making the fading of the "exaggeration" less pronounced, step-to-step, and minimizing or avoiding student errors.

The upper right of Figure 5.3 is an example of an extra stimulus prompt (i.e., it is called *extra* because a cue is *added* to the training item, in this case, a background color that cues the learner to the correct answer). Over consecutive correct responses this background color is faded (i.e., made less pronounced) until the background is the same for all the training items. As with the within stimulus prompt, discussed above, should the student make errors, the teacher can adjust by adding additional fading steps. This minimizes the "jump" from one step to another, in terms of difference in the level of background color. This avoids errors and makes the transfer of control of student responding from the prompt to the target items smoother and more gradual.

The bottom two examples illustrate pairing a known item (e.g., the picture of a cup; the numeral 3) with a new, to-be-learned item (e.g., the printed word C-U-P and dots representing the amount three, respectively). The goal of such pairing is to transfer control of responding from the known item that initially was followed by correct student responding to the new item (e.g., the printed word C-U-P and the dots representing the amount three). This is accomplished by gradually and systematically fading out the known items, contingent on consecutive correct student responses. As with the other examples already presented, the number of fading steps can be adjusted to meet the specific needs of each student.

Interestingly, an equivalence study by Palmer et al. (2020) combined errorless instruction with the use of complex stimuli. In that study, each individual class was established by using a color prompt during teaching, with a different color being associated with each different class. The color highlighted the correct choice and was gradually faded, based on continued student correct responding, until the target item controlled accurate learner responding in the absence of the color prompt. Not only were the initial relations trained with few errors but all the new, untaught relations emerged, the three classes formed, and the different colors (prompts) were documented as members of their related equivalence classes.

Some benefits of using an errorless approach to skill acquisition include the increased probability that the learner will receive positive feedback for correct answers when compared to typical trial-and-error and error-correction-alone procedures. This increase in positive feedback (i.e., reinforcement) for correct responses may also be associated with higher motivation for learning. Another benefit of errorless instruction is potential reduction in negative responses such as frustration and challenging behaviors as a result of errors and corrective procedures.

Issues with training are one of the primary explanations when learners do not demonstrate emergent relations during tests for equivalence. Establishing those baseline (i.e., initial) relations via errorless instruction may ameliorate training issues and potentially facilitate equivalence-class formation, thereby enhancing equivalence-based instruction.

Recommendations

1   Where possible, teach using multiple-element items as it will decrease the number of teaching trials and the time devoted to teaching.
2   Teach the initial relations via a many-to-one method (Chapter 4).
3   Use a teaching procedure that limits learner errors (i.e., errorless learning).

References

Bondy, A. S., & Frost, L. A. (1998). The picture exchange communication system. *Seminars in Speech and Language*, *19*, 373–389.

Cooper, J. O., Heron, T. E., & Heward, W. L. (2020). *Applied behavior analysis* (3rd ed.). Pearson.

Dube, W. V. (2009). Stimulus overselectivity in discrimination learning. In P. Reed (Ed.), *Behavioural theories and interventions for autism* (pp. 23–46). Nova Science Publishers.

Dube, W. V., & Wilkinson, K. M. (2014). The potential influence of stimulus overselectivity in AAC: Information from eye tracking and behavioral studies of attention with individuals with intellectual disabilities. *Augmentative and Alternative Communication*, *30*, 172–185. https://doi.org/10.3109/07434618.2014.904924. PMID: 24773053; PMCID: PMC4047139

Etzel, B. C., & LeBlanc, J. M. (1979). The simplest treatment alternative: The law of parsimony applied to choosing appropriate instructional control and errorless-learning procedures for the difficult-to-teach children. *Journal of Autism and Developmental Disorders*, *9*, 361–382. https://doi.org/10.1007/BF01531445

Farber, R. S., Dube, W. V., & Dickson, C. A. (2016). A sorting-to-matching method to teach compound matching to sample. *Journal of Applied Behavior Analysis*, *49*(2), 294–307. https://doi.org/10.1002/jaba.290

Green, G. (2001). Behavior analytic instruction for learners with autism: Advances in stimulus control technology. *Focus on Autism and Other*

Developmental Disabilities, 16(2), 72–85. https://doi.org/10.1177/1088 35760101600203

Groskreutz, N. C., Karsina, A., Miguel, C. F., & Groskreutz, M. P. (2010). Using complex auditory-visual samples to produce emergent relations in children with autism. *Journal of Applied Behavior Analysis, 43*(1), 131–136. https://doi.org/10.1901/jaba.2010.43-131

Hume, K., Loftin, R., & Lantz, J. (2009). Increasing independence in autism spectrum disorders: A review of three focused interventions. *Journal of Autism and Developmental Disorders, 39,* 1329–1338.

Lancioni, G. E., & Smeets, P. M. (1986). Procedures and parameters of error-less discrimination training with developmentally impaired individuals. In N. R. Ellis & N. W. Bray (Eds.), *International review of research in mental retardation* (pp. 135–164). Academic Press.

Litrownik, A. J., McInnis, E. T., Wetzel-Pritchard, A., & Filipelli, D. L. (1978). Restricted stimulus control and inferred attentional deficits in autistic and retarded children. *Journal of Abnormal Psychology, 87*(5), 554–562. https://doi.org/10.1037/0021-843X.87.5.554

Lovaas, O. I., Schreibman, L., Koegel, R., & Rehm, R. (1971). Selective respond-ing by autistic children to multiple sensory input. *Journal of Abnormal Psy-chology, 77*(3), 211–222. https://doi.org/10.1037/h0031015

MacDuff, G. S., Krantz, P. J., & McClannahan, L. E. (2001). Prompts and prompt-fading strategies for people with autism. In C. Maurice, G. Green, & R. M. Foxx (Eds.), *Making a difference: Behavior Intervention for Autism.* PRO-ED.

Maguire, R. W., Breault, M., Yorlets, C., & King, C. M. (2018). Comparison of an errorless learning to a trial-and-error protocol on equivalence class for-mation. Paper presented at the Conference of the Association of Behavior Analysis International, San Diego, CA.

Maguire, R. W., Holcomb, W. L., Gould, K. E., & Bass, R. (1988). The effects of errors during training on the formation of stimulus classes. In R. W. Maguire (Chair) *The Effects of Errors on the Acquisition of Conditional Discriminations and Stimulus Class Formation: Analysis and Intervention.* Paper presented at the Association for Behavior Analysis, Philadel-phia, PA.

Maguire, R. W., Stromer, R., & Mackay, H. A. (1995). Delayed matching to complex samples and the formation of stimulus classes in children. *Psy-chological Reports, 77,* 1059–1076.

Maguire, R. W., Stromer, R., Mackay, H. A., & Demis, C. A. (1994). Matching to complex samples and stimulus class formation in adults with autism and young children. *Journal of Autism and Developmental Disorders, 24*(6), 753–772. https://doi.org/10.1007/BF02172284

MacDuff, G. S., Krantz, P. J., & McClannahan, L. E. (2001). Prompts and prompt-fading strategies for people with autism. In C. Maurice, G.

Green, & R. M. Foxx (Eds.), *Making a difference: Behavioral intervention for autism* (pp. 37–50). PRO-ED.

O'Neill, S. J., McDowell, C., & Leslie, J. C. (2018). A comparison of prompt delays with trial-and-error instruction in conditional discrimination training. *Behavior Analysis in Practice, 11*(4), 370–380. https://doi.org/10.1007/s40617-018-0261-9

Palmer, S. K., Maguire, R. W., Lionello-DeNolf, K., & Braga-Kenyon, P. (2020). The inclusion of prompts in equivalence classes. *Journal of the Experimental Analysis of Behavior, 115*(1), 255–271. https://doi.org/10.1002/jeab.655

Rosales, R., Maderitz, C., & Garcia, Y. A. (2014). Comparison of simple and complex auditory-visual conditional discrimination training. *Journal of Applied Behavior Analysis, 47*, 1–6. https://doi.org/10.1002/jaba.121

Sidman, M. (1971). Reading and auditory-visual equivalences. *Journal of Speech and Hearing Research, 14*, 5–13. https://doi.org/10.1044/jshr.1401.05

Sidman, M., & Stoddard, L. T. (1966). Programming perception and learning for retarded children. In N. R. Ellis (Ed.), *International Review of Research in Mental Retardation* (Vol. 2, pp. 151–208). Academic Press.

Stromer, R., McIlvane, W. J., Dube, W. V., & Mackay, H. A. (1993). Assessing control by elements of complex stimuli in delayed matching to sample. *Journal of the Experimental Analysis of Behavior, 59*(1), 83–102. https://doi.org/10.1901/jeab.1993.59-83

Stromer, R., & Stromer, J. B. (1990a). The formation of arbitrary stimulus classes in matching to complex samples. *The Psychological Record, 40*, 51–66. https://doi.org/10.1007/BF03399571

Stromer, R., & Stromer, J. B. (1990b). Matching to complex samples: Further study of arbitrary stimulus classes. *Psychological Record, 40*, 505–516. https://doi.org/10.1007/BF03399537

Terrace, H. S. (1963a). Discrimination learning with and without errors. *Journal of the Experimental Analysis of Behavior, 6*, 1–27.

Terrace, H. S. (1963b). Errorless transfer of a discrimination across two continua. *Journal of the Experimental Analysis of Behavior, 6*, 223–232.

Touchette, P. E. (1971). Transfer of stimulus control: Measuring the moment of transfer. *Journal of the Experimental Analysis of Behavior, 15*, 347–354.

Touchette, P. E., & Howard, J. S. (1984). Errorless learning: Reinforcement contingencies and stimulus control transfer in delayed prompting. *Journal of Applied Behavior Analysis, 17*, 175–188.

Yorlets, C. B., Maguire, R. W., King, C. M., & Breault, M. (2018). Acquisition of complex conditional discriminations in a child with autism spectrum disorder. *The Psychological Record, 68*(2), 219–229. https://doi.org/10.1007/s40732-018-0283-2

6

Equivalence and Differential Outcomes

Colleen Yorlets

The term *outcomes* is used to refer to the reinforcer element of the contingency (Peterson & Trapold, 1980). Differential outcomes has been defined as the application of a unique reinforcer for each skill being taught (Mok et al., 2010). For example, when playing the piano each of the 88 keys produces a unique sound when one key is pressed versus the sound made when a different key is pressed. *Common outcomes* has been defined as the application of the same reinforcer following each of a variety of different skills (Mok et al., 2010). For example, clicking a clicker every time your dog complies with a command. Table 6.1 provides an example of teaching using common outcomes. In this example, three different relations are being taught, each of which is a member of different classes. The consequence for responding correctly for all three relations is, however, the same. If the learner correctly matches Boston to Massachusetts, Boise to Idaho, and Bismarck to North Dakota, the teacher will compliment all three responses with the same "good job."

Differential outcomes is used to refer to arrangements in which unique reinforcers are used for different classes (i.e., groups) of stimuli (i.e., items) (Mok et al., 2010). An example of *differential outcomes* is shown in Table 6.2. Again, three different relations are being taught. When using differential outcomes, each relation has a different, unique reinforcer delivered following correct responding. For example, if a learner matches Boston to Massachusetts, a correct response may be reinforced with a picture of the black-capped chickadee (state bird of Massachusetts, State Symbols USA, n.d.). Correctly matching Boise to Idaho, on the other hand, is reinforced with a picture of

DOI: 10.4324/9781003297161-6

Table 6.1 Three Different Matching-to-Sample Targets and Responses with a Common Outcome

Elements	Teaching Target 1	Teaching Target 2	Teaching Target 3
Sample	Massachusetts	North Dakota	Idaho
Comparisons	Bismarck Boise Boston	Boise Boston Bismarck	Boston Bismarck Boise
Response Reinforcer	Select Boston "Good job!"	Select Bismarck "Good job!"	Select Boise "Good job!"

Table 6.2 Three Different Matching-to-Sample Targets and Responses with Related Differential Outcomes

Elements	Teaching Target 1	Teaching Target 2	Teaching Target 3
Sample	Massachusetts	North Dakota	Idaho
Comparisons	Bismarck Boise Boston	Boise Boston Bismarck	Boston Bismarck Boise
Response Reinforcer	Select Boston Picture of Black-capped Chickadee	Select Bismarck Picture of Western Meadowlark	Select Boise Picture of Mountain Bluebird

the mountain bluebird (state bird of Idaho, State Symbols USA, n.d.). Lastly, matching Bismarck to North Dakota is reinforced with a picture of the western meadowlark (state bird of North Dakota, State Symbols USA, n.d.). So, for each different relation being taught, a different reinforcer is used. Reinforcers are unique to these relations in that they do not change. Every time Boston is matched to Massachusetts, the picture of the black-capped chickadee is presented, and the same for the other relations, using their unique reinforcers.

One of the most important benefits to using differential outcomes may be an increase in the rate of skill acquisition (McCormack et al., 2017; McCormack et al., 2019, 2021). This is often measured by the number of trials or sessions to acquire the skills being taught (Peterson & Trapold, 1980). Although the difference between differential outcomes and common outcomes may be minor when teaching a single skill, the differences may be much greater if teaching multiple skills (McCormack et al., 2021). If the differential outcomes procedure results in acquisition in one or two fewer sessions than other reinforcer arrangements, the number of sessions saved begins to quickly multiply (McCormack et al., 2021).

Unique reinforcers may also become part of a stimulus class (Sidman, 2000). This result means that the stimulus class is enlarged to include an additional member (Sidman, 2000). In most cases, if correctly designed, class expansion will occur (Maguire et al., 1994; Palmer et al., 2021). Additionally, it may be possible to select reinforcers that are already related to the academic items under real-world conditions. For example, when teaching a learner to match a picture of a block and the printed word B-L-O-C-K to the spoken word "block," a reinforcer of a physical block may create a naturally occurring stimulus class.

The first documented instance of the differential outcomes effect may be Trapold's 1970 study conducted with rats. Two levers were present: pressing the right lever was reinforced in the presence of a tone and pressing the left lever was reinforced in the presence of a clicker. Also, different, unique reinforcers were delivered for responding correctly to the tone and clicker (e.g., food and sucrose). A higher rate of responding was demonstrated for rats whose lever-pressing was reinforced by a unique consequence, as compared to those who received a common reinforcer (Trapold, 1970). This study illustrated the potential positive effects of using differential outcomes, rather than common outcomes, when teaching new skills.

Malanga and Poling's 1992 study may be the first in which the differential outcomes effect was demonstrated in adults. The participants were four adults diagnosed with intellectual disabilities. Participants were presented with several pairs of static pictures of American Sign Language (ASL) letters and instructed to touch a sign. In the differential outcomes condition, correctly selecting each letter was followed by a unique consequence, either food or verbal praise. Results demonstrated that the differential outcomes condition resulted in the highest average accuracy of responding (Malanga & Poling, 1992).

Several other applied studies have been conducted with different populations in which the differential outcomes effect (DOE) has been demonstrated. McCormack et al. (2017) showed evidence of the DOE for two out of three children diagnosed with autism, for tact (name) training. McCormack et al. (2021) demonstrated the DOE for children diagnosed with intellectual or developmental disabilities, again for tact (name) training. Conditional discrimination training was conducted for adults and children diagnosed with Down syndrome using differential outcomes and found to be effective (Estévez et al., 2003).

The differential outcomes procedure may be beneficial when student response accuracy during teaching is low (Estévez, 2005; McCormack et al., 2021). McCormack et al. (2017) cautioned that there may be a ceiling effect with very accurate student performances (e.g., the impact may be minimal). Also, differential outcomes may be associated with better student outcomes when task difficulty increases or when new academic items are introduced (Estévez et al., 2001; Goeters et al., 1992; McCormack et al., 2017; McCormack et al., 2019).

Reinforcer Selection

Quality

Perhaps the most important parameter of reinforcement is its quality (e.g., the accelerative impact on behavior). When the same reinforcers are used to teach different skills (common outcomes) they are assumed to be the same quality. However, if different reinforcers are used for each different skill, they may or may not be equally effective (Litt & Schreibman, 1981; McCormack et al., 2017). If one reinforcer is of a higher quality than another, the learner may respond more frequently to the items associated with the highest-quality reinforcer, relative to items associated with other reinforcers (McCormack et al., 2017). Further, while differential outcomes have been shown to produce quicker, more accurate skill acquisition, this may not be demonstrated if reinforcers are of different quality (Litt & Schreibman, 1981; McCormack et al., 2017).

In a number of studies, a reinforcer assessment was done at the outset, prior to conducting any training (Chong & Carr, 2010; Dube et al., 1987; Dube et al., 1989). Dube et al. (1987, 1989) conducted what they referred to as "reinforcer-preference testing." In their studies, food items were used as reinforcers (Dube et al., 1987, 1989). As part of the reinforcer-preference testing, two food items were presented on each trial. All combinations of the four food items being assessed were presented (Dube et al., 1987, 1989). They then used as reinforcers the two food items that were selected approximately the same number of times (Dube et al., 1987, 1989).

Chong and Carr (2010) first had parents complete a survey (Fisher et al., 1996) to identify possible preferences. Then they conducted a paired-stimulus preference assessment (Fisher et al., 1992), which resulted in a rank-ordering of items. A multiple-stimulus-without-replacement preference assessment was conducted daily to assess the highest ranked items (Chong & Carr, 2010).

McCormack et al. (2017) also had parents complete a survey (Reinforcer Assessment for Individuals with Disabilities) (Fisher et al., 1996), and then conducted a paired stimulus preference assessment. McCormack and colleagues only utilized items as reinforcers which had been selected for greater than 50% of opportunities and for which the percent of trials selected was no more than a 10% difference from the other items. This was done to minimize the possibility of using reinforcers of markedly different qualities (McCormack et al., 2017). The use of preference and reinforcer assessments may help to ensure selection of items that are likely to function as reinforcers.

Delivery and Consumption

Even when the different reinforcers to be used have been documented to be comparable, there are still other considerations to take into account to ensure the best outcomes possible. For example, reinforcers should be selected that can be delivered and consumed quickly. There are a number of benefits to maintaining a quick pace of instruction, including reducing the occurrence of problem behavior (Roxburgh & Carbone, 2013). It is also important to consider the likelihood of satiation (i.e., loss of reinforcing properties due to too frequent use). It may be beneficial to collect some data on the rate of trial presentation to be able to, roughly, estimate how many reinforcers may be delivered within a certain period of time. Doing so may help to guide reinforcer selection, as learners may satiate quickly on certain types of stimuli.

As previously noted, the importance of selecting reinforcers that are comparable cannot be overstated (Litt & Schreibman, 1981; McCormack et al., 2017). Litt and Schreibman (1981) demonstrated this when comparing high-quality reinforcers with lower-quality reinforcers. Correctly selecting an object was followed by access to a reinforcer, one high-quality and one lower-quality. Each object was associated with the same reinforcer across all trials. Then the reinforcers associated with each object were switched so that the object previously associated with the lower-quality reinforcer was now associated with the higher-quality reinforcer, and vice versa. In both conditions, experimenters found that accuracy of responding was consistently highest for the object associated with the higher-quality reinforcer. Accuracy of responding for objects associated with the lower-quality reinforcer, however, remained at mid-to-low levels (Litt & Schreibman, 1981).

McCormack et al. (2017) reported findings consistent with Litt and Schreibman (1981). They conducted a study in which each participant was taught skills comparing differential and non-differential outcomes. Two of the three participants demonstrated increased accuracy and fewer sessions to criterion in the differential outcomes (DO) condition, as compared to the non-differential outcomes (NDO) condition. Interestingly, for Participant 3, mastery was only achieved within the NDO condition. Researchers found that Participant 3 responded to the item that was associated with the high-quality reinforcer (McCormack et al., 2017).

Number of Reinforcers

When using differential outcomes, because each potential stimulus class to be formed requires its own unique reinforcer, teachers must identify more reinforcers than if common reinforcers were being used (McCormack et al., 2021). It may already be challenging to identify reinforcers for some learners and so increasing the number needed may further exacerbate this challenge (McCormack et al., 2021).

In an effort to overcome the challenge of finding multiple reinforcers, Estévez et al. (2003) used red and green tokens (differential outcomes) to teach matching tasks to 24 individuals, ages 6–37, diagnosed with Down syndrome. Correct responses were followed by either a red or green token. Red tokens could be exchanged for food, whereas green tokens were exchanged for toys. Overall, Estévez and colleagues found that the differential outcomes condition, relative to the non-differential outcomes condition, resulted in an increased rate of learning and accuracy (Estévez et al., 2003). Although utilizing tokens may ameliorate some of the challenges of identifying sufficiently equal-quality reinforcers, one thing to keep in mind is that tokens must first be conditioned to function as reinforcers (Cooper et al., 2020). McCormack et al. (2021) proposed another strategy for easing the task of reinforcer selection, while using equal-quality reinforcers. They assessed if variations of documented reinforcers could serve as unique reinforcers. Following a parent survey, McCormack et al. (2021) conducted a multiple-stimulus-without-replacement preference assessment with different versions of the same item and confirmed that different forms of the same potential reinforcer (e.g., wind-up fan and electric fan) were selected a similar number of times.

Relation to Classes

Something important to remember when using differential outcomes is, if all goes as planned, that the reinforcers may become part of the stimulus class, meaning that they will be related to the other items in the class (Sidman, 2000). To assist in this process, it may be possible to select items as reinforcers that are thematically related to relations being trained (Pilgrim et al., 2000). For example, in Table 6.2 the reinforcers were all pictures of different state birds. Although these items are being called *reinforcers*, they need to actually be proven to function as reinforcers. However, it may not always be possible to identify unique items that function as reinforcers *and* are thematically related to the other items. If this is the case, one may use unrelated and different reinforcers as in Table 6.3.

Table 6.3 Three Different Matching-to-Sample Targets and Responses with Unrelated Differential Outcomes

Elements	Teaching Target 1	Teaching Target 2	Teaching Target 3
Sample	Massachusetts	North Dakota	Idaho
Comparisons	Bismarck Boise Boston	Boise Boston Bismarck	Boston Bismarck Boise
Response	Select Boston	Select Bismarck	Select Boise
Reinforcer	Play-doh	Glow Stick	Slinky

Instructional Plan

Particularly important in the planning process is the consideration of whether to use a tabletop presentation or some type of electronic means. Initial considerations include:

The learner's prerequisite skills: The learner's prerequisite skills and learner history with previous instructional presentations may guide the format of instruction (Green, 2001). Are there certain modes of presentation that are best suited for the learner based on skill, history, or preference?

Resources: Another factor is what resources are consistently available. For example, if a computer is not consistently available for sessions, then a tabletop presentation would be best.

Preparation: Assess the resources necessary to prepare the instructional materials. If physical resources are not a barrier, you might consider which set of materials (e.g., computer-based vs. tabletop), will require the least amount of time to develop. Resources considered should also include the teacher-to-learner ratio. If, for example, the learner will be expected to complete this task in a small-group setting, they may be required to complete the task with some level of independence.

There are benefits and limitations to using tabletop and computer-based instruction. In tabletop instruction, no electronic device or technology skills are required. Computer-based instruction may allow for some types of consequences to be programmed into the software and such software may even collect data (Goldsmith & LeBlanc, 2004). Technology may not always be available, can malfunction, and will not be feasible for all types of items. All of that being said, both tabletop (e.g., Malanga & Poling, 1992) and computer-based instruction (e.g., Dube et al., 1989) can be effective, so teachers and learners are not limited if they use one as opposed to another.

Data Collection

In order to evaluate the effectiveness of the procedures used, data must be collected. The data sheet being used, therefore, is important and can be used to facilitate accurate trial presentation, response scoring, and the unique reinforcers used. We suggest using a data sheet similar to the one displayed in Figure 6.1. This data sheet specifies not only the stimuli to be matched to one another, if using a matching-to-sample format, but also the unique reinforcers to be delivered for correct responding on each trial. Keeping track of the

Trial	Sample Printed Words		Comparisons (Note: printed words shown here rather than icons)			Differential Outcomes
			Left	Middle	Right	
1	D-O-G		Pig	Cow	Dog	Juice
2	C-O-W		Dog	Cow	Pig	M&M
3	P-I-G		Pig	Dog	Cow	Yogurt
4	C-O-W		Pig	Cow	Dog	M&M
5	D-O-G		Cow	Pig	Dog	Juice
6	C-O-W		Cow	Dog	Pig	M&M
7	P-I-G		Dog	Pig	Cow	Yogurt
8	C-O-W		Cow	Pig	Dog	M&M
9	P-I-G		Dog	Cow	Pig	Yogurt
10	D-O-G		Cow	Dog	Pig	Juice
11	C-O-W		Pig	Dog	Cow	M&M
12	D-O-G		Dog	Cow	Pig	Juice
13	P-I-G		Cow	Dog	Pig	Yogurt
14	D-O-G		Dog	Pig	Cow	Juice
15	P-I-G		Cow	Pig	Dog	Yogurt
16	C-O-W		Dog	Pig	Cow	M&M
17	D-O-G		Pig	Dog	Cow	Juice
18	P-I-G		Pig	Cow	Dog	Yogurt

Figure 6.1 Sample Teaching Data Sheet with Differential Outcomes

unique reinforcer to be delivered can be challenging when utilizing differential outcomes, so the data sheet will help with this. The data sheet should be individualized with the specific stimuli being used (items to be taught, reinforcers), to help facilitate a quick pace of presentation. As previously noted (Chapter 4) the use of data sheets, such as provided in Figure 6.1, allows the teacher to circle the student's response, instead of merely noting a correct versus an incorrect answer. This will allow the teacher to conduct a trial-by-trial error analysis to determine if any confounds (bias variables) influenced student answers (e.g., stimulus position or item or reinforcer preferences; Dickson et al., 2006).

Practice

Once materials are prepared, we suggest practicing a bit without the learner present. If using computer-based instruction, especially if there are any videos, animations, or transitions included, it is wise to test these in advance to ensure that all components are working properly. If presenting via tabletop, it is helpful to practice presenting the materials, including the correct reinforcer, while maintaining a good pace. As always, organization of materials is important to ensure that they are easily accessible. If any environmental manipulations need to be made based on the learner's behaviors (e.g., swiping materials off the table), these should be factored in as well.

Error Prevention

The impact of errors on learners can be detrimental and result in more errors (Green, 2001). Given this, it's important that training be conducted with as few errors as possible (Green, 2001). Using an errorless learning procedure and following a written plan are two steps that can be taken toward that goal (see Chapters 4 and 5).

Testing for Emergence

Once training mastery has been obtained, you will test for the emergence of relations that were not directly trained. If emergence is not immediately forthcoming (delayed emergence, Sidman, 1994), retesting and retraining may remedy this issue (see Chapter 4).

Limitations

Although there is an increasing number of applied studies that demonstrate the efficacy of differential outcomes (Estévez et al., 2003; Malanga & Poling, 1992; McCormack et al., 2021; Miller et al., 2002), the effect has not always been demonstrated (Chong & Carr, 2010). Thus, there is a continued need to research this area (McCormack et al., 2017; McCormack et al., 2021).

Additionally, requirements for the differential outcomes procedure may prove especially challenging for learners with limited reinforcers (McCormack et al., 2019). Each class of stimuli must be assigned its own unique reinforcer, and these reinforcers must be of about the same quality. This requirement may eliminate potential reinforcers that would otherwise be utilized (McCormack et al., 2019). In this instance, the use of tokens (Estévez et al., 2003) or different versions of the same reinforcer (McCormack et al., 2021) should be considered.

Regardless, Urcuioli (1990, p. 410) referred to the DOE as very "powerful" and this procedure should be considered, not just with equivalence-based instruction, but for all instruction.

References

Chong, I. M., & Carr, J. E. (2010). Failure to demonstrate the differential outcomes effect in children with autism. *Behavioral Interventions*, 25(4), 339–348. https://doi.org/10.1002/bin.318

Dickson, C. A., Wang, S. S., Lombard, K. M., & Dube, W. V. (2006). Overselective stimulus control in residential school students with intellectual disabilities. *Research in Developmental Disabilities, 27*(6), 618–631. https://doi.org/10.1016/j.ridd.2005.07.004

Dube, W. V., McIlvane, W. J., Mackay, H. A., & Stoddard, L. T. (1987). Stimulus class membership established via stimulus-reinforcer relations. *Journal of the Experimental Analysis of Behavior, 47*(2), 159–175. https://doi.org/10.1901/jeab.1987.47-159

Dube, W. V., McIlvane, W. J., Maguire, R. W., Mackay, H. A., & Stoddard, L. T. (1989). Stimulus class formation and stimulus-reinforcer relations. *Journal of the Experimental Analysis of Behavior, 51*(1), 65–76. https://doi.org/10.1901/jeab.1989.51-65

Estévez, A. F. (2005). The differential outcomes effect: A useful tool to improve discriminative learning in humans. *The Behavior Analyst Today, 6*(4), 216–220. https://doi.org/10.1037/h0100079

Estévez, A. F., Fuentes, L. J., Marí-Bêffa, P., González, C., & Alvarez, D. (2001). The differential outcomes effect as a useful tool to improve conditional discrimination learning in children. *Learning and Motivation, 32*(1), 48–64. https://doi.org/10.1006/lmot.2000.1060

Estévez, A. F., Fuentes, L. J., Overmier, J. B., & González, C. (2003). Differential outcomes effect in children and adults with Down syndrome. *American Journal on Mental Retardation, 108*(2), 108–116. https://doi.org/10.1352/0895-8017(2003)108<0108:DOEICA>2.0.CO;2

Fisher, W. W., Piazza, C., Bowman, L. G., & Amari, A. (1996). Integrating caregiver report with a systematic choice assessment to enhance reinforcer identification. *American Journal on Mental Retardation, 101*(10), 15–25.

Fisher, W. W., Piazza, C. C., Bowman, L. G., Hagopian, L. P., Owens, J. C., & Slevin, I. (1992). A comparison of two approaches for identifying reinforcers for persons with severe and profound disabilities. *Journal of Applied Behavior Analysis, 25*(2), 491–498. https://doi.org/10.1901/jaba.1992.25-491

Goeters, S., Blakely, E., & Poling, A. (1992). The differential outcomes effect. *The Psychological Record, 42*(3), 389–411. https://doi.org/10.1007/BF03399609

Goldsmith, T. R., & LeBlanc, L. A. (2004). Use of technology in interventions for children with autism. *Journal of Early and Intensive Behavior Intervention, 1*(2), 166–178. https://doi.org/10.1037/h0100287

Green, G. (2001). Behavior analytic instruction for learners with autism: Advances in stimulus control technology. *Focus on Autism and Other Developmental Disabilities, 16*(2), 72–85. https://doi.org/10.1177/108835760101600203

Litt, M. D., & Schreibman, L. (1981). Stimulus-specific reinforcement in the acquisition of receptive labels by autistic children. *Analysis and Intervention in Developmental Disabilities, 1*(2), 171–186. https://doi.org/10.1016/0270-4684(81)90030-6

Maguire, R. W., Stromer, R., Mackay, H. A., & Demis, C. A. (1994). Matching to complex samples and stimulus class formation in adults with autism and young children. *Journal of Autism and Developmental Disorders, 24*(6), 753–772. https://doi.org/10.1007/BF02172284

Malanga, P., & Poling, A. (1992). Letter recognition by adults with mental handicaps: Improving performance through differential outcomes. *Developmental Disabilities Bulletin, 20*(2), 18–38.

McCormack, J., Arnold-Saritepe, A., & Elliffe, D. (2017). The differential outcomes effect in children with autism. *Behavioral Interventions, 32*(4), 357–369. https://doi.org/10.1002/bin.1489

McCormack, J. C., Elliffe, D., & Virués-Ortega, J. (2019). Quantifying the effects of the differential outcomes procedure in humans: A systematic review and a meta-analysis. *Journal of Applied Behavior Analysis, 52*(3), 870–892. https://doi.org/10.1002/jaba.578

McCormack, J. C., Elliffe, D., & Virués-Ortega, J. (2021). Enhanced tact acquisition using the differential outcomes procedure in children with developmental and intellectual disability. *The Psychological Record, 71*(1), 55–70. https://doi.org/10.1007/s40732-020-00429-8

Miller, O. T., Waugh, K. M., & Chambers, K. (2002). Differential outcomes effect: Increased accuracy in adults learning kanji with stimulus specific rewards. *The Psychological Record, 52*(3), 315–324. https://doi.org/10.1007/BF03395433

Mok, L. W., Estévez, A. F., & Overmier, J. B. (2010). Unique outcome expectations as a training and pedagogical tool. *The Psychological Record, 60*(2), 227–248. https://doi.org/10.1007/BF03395705

Palmer, S. K., Maguire, R. W., Lionello-DeNolf, K. M., & Braga-Kenyon, P. (2021). Expansion of Sidman's theory: The inclusion of prompt stimuli in equivalence classes. *Journal of the Experimental Analysis of Behavior, 115*(1), 255–271. https://doi.org/10.1002/jeab.655

Peterson, G. B., & Trapold, M. A. (1980). Effects of altering outcome expectancies on pigeons' delayed conditional discrimination performance. *Learning and Motivation, 11*(3), 267–288. https://doi.org/10.1016/0023-9690(80)90001-6

Pilgrim, C., Jackson, J., & Galizio, M. (2000). Acquisition of arbitrary conditional discriminations by young normally developing children. *Journal of the Experimental Analysis of Behavior, 73*(2), 177–193. https://doi.org/10.1901/jeab.2000.73-177

Roxburgh, C. A., & Carbone, V. J. (2013). The effect of varying teacher presentation rates on responding during discrete trial training for two children with autism. *Behavior Modification*, *37*(3), 298–323. https://doi.org/10.1177%2F0145445512463046

Sidman, M. (1994). *Equivalence relations and behavior: A research story.* Authors Cooperative, Inc.

Sidman, M. (2000). Equivalence relations and the reinforcement contingency. *Journal of the Experimental Analysis of Behavior*, *74*(1), 127–146. https://doi.org/10.1901/jeab.2000.74-127

State Symbols USA. (n.d.). *State birds.* https://statesymbolsusa.org/categories/bird

Trapold, M. A. (1970). Are expectancies based upon different positive reinforcing events discriminably different? *Learning and Motivation*, *1*(2), 129–140. https://doi.org/10.1016/0023-9690(70)90079-2

Urcuioli, P. J. (1990). Some relationships between outcome expectancies and sample stimuli in pigeons' delayed matching. *Animal Learning & Behavior*, *18*(3), 302–314. https://doi.org/10.3758/BF03205290

7

Equivalence and Verbal Behavior

Christina M. King

One of the most exciting times in the life of a parent of a young child is when they watch language develop. In most cases, the child first begins to use their voice to produce vocalizations that correspond to specific things in the environment and many parents are amazed by their child's learning. Particularly amazing is when these new skills occur despite not having been directly taught. How is the child learning the names of items? How are they learning to ask for things they want or reject things they don't? And how are they learning to follow directions?

Unfortunately, there are also many children who do not acquire language easily and require intervention. Children who do not acquire language at the same rate as their typically developing peers may display more undesired behaviors, may be more dependent on caregivers, and may not acquire other skills, such as academic and social skills. Although there is a good deal of research investigating and proposing various theories of language development, there are noticeable research-to-practice gaps. Teachers are often tasked with teaching language to students with special needs, but the relevant research may be difficult to interpret and may not allow for easy application. In this chapter, an overview of language-based terminology and equivalence-based instruction procedures used to teach language efficiently and effectively will be outlined.

Language Acquisition

In *Verbal Behavior* (1957), Skinner proposed a behavioral theory of language acquisition. According to Skinner, language is behavior, no different than any

DOI: 10.4324/9781003297161-7

other kind of behavior, in that it can be taught and brought under control of the environment in which it occurs. Skinner identified categories of language such as the mand, tact, and listener behavior. The first two categories correspond to expressive language and the last category corresponds to what is traditionally referred to as receptive language. A *mand* can be thought of as a request or demand. Reinforcement for the mand is access to the requested item or action. A *tact* is the behavior of labeling or naming an item. Receptive language or listener behavior is when one responds to another person's language by selecting an item that corresponds to that person's statement (e.g., touching the color red after the teacher says "Touch red").

One of the important aspects of Skinner's (1957) conception of language development is that a word (e.g., "water") may be acquired in one context (e.g., a mand, "Give me some water"), but may not occur in a different context (e.g., a tact, "I see water"). However, as a child continues in language development they quickly learn to *request* an item and then when asked "What is it?" they are able to supply the name of the item. Also, when asked to *receptively* act upon or find that item, they may be able to point to it or go and retrieve that item. So, the further developed child may first learn a word under one set of circumstances, in this case a request, and then be able to display it under different conditions (e.g., label or find). But, how does this occur? An example may prove illustrative.

We conducted a study documenting the transfer of mastered skills from one set of circumstances to another, via equivalence-based instruction (King, 2016). Two typically developing preschool children were taught to name two items, each from three different categories of nonsense words and pictures. Table 7.1 presents the items used in the study. Class 1 was the "Cugs" class, Class 2 was the "Veks" class and Class 3 was the "Zids" class. Each consisted of two different nonsense forms (B and C items) and a spoken name, by the child.

The students were first taught to name (i.e., cug, vek or zid) the items. Once they learned to name each item within the same potential class, they were tested to see if they could match the two different items to one another.

Table 7.1 Items Used During Name Training

Potential Class	B-Items	C-Items	Name Item
1	▓	⚖	"cug"
2	◯	§	"vek"
3	◈	╬	"zid"

For example, could they match the B-item and C-item in the category of "cug" to one another, even though they had not been taught to do so? Also, the children were assessed to determine if they could select items by the name of that item, when spoken by the teacher (i.e. "find the cug"). Again, this skill had not been taught. This required the introduction of a new item or stimulus, the teacher's spoken direction "Find the ____" (A-items). Table 7.2 presents all the items used in the aspect of the study.

Remarkably, both children matched the B and C items, from the same class, to one another *AND* selected the B and C after the teacher said "Touch ____," even though these skills had not been taught (i.e., they emerged without direct instruction). This is comparable to the emerging or untaught language skills of children.

Building on these newly emergent skills, the children were then taught to match a new item, D, to the B-items. Following this instruction, the student's abilities to match the B, C and D items to one another *AND* select D-items following the teacher saying "Touch ____" was assessed. Both students were able to match all the items within a potential class to each other and select D-items following the teacher's spoken direction to do so. It is important to note that during instruction of matching D items to B items, the spoken names

Table 7.2 Items Used During the Potential Expansion of the Classes to Include A-items

Potential Class	A-Item (spoken by the teacher)	B-Items	C-Items	Name Item
1	"cug"	▦	⏛	Child says "cug"
2	"vek"	◯	§	Child says "vek"
3	"zid"	◉	⊥⊤	Child says "zid"

Table 7.3 Items Used During the Potential Expansion of the Classes to Include D-Items

Potential Class	A-Item (spoken by the teacher)	B-Item	C-Item	D-Item	Name Item
1	"cug"	▦	⏛	₪	Child says "cug"
2	"vek"	◯	§	Ж	Child says "vek"
3	"zid"	◉	⊥⊤	Ю	Child says "zid"

associated with the class (e.g., "cug," "vek," "zid") were never presented (only the B, C, and D symbols were paired without the class name). Thus, the D-C, C-D and C-B matching emerged in the absence of teaching, as did the selection of D-items following the teacher's spoken direction.

Lastly, the students were taught to construct three different sequences of the items within each class (B, C and D items), with one missing. In order to complete the sequence, the students needed to ask for the missing item. Requesting (manding) the missing item emerged for both students, despite such actions never having been taught. Table 7.4 presents the items used in this part of the study.

In summary, children were taught to name two items from each class and then match a third item to one item from the class. As a result, the children demonstrated the following skills in the absence of teaching:

◆ select all items following the teacher's spoken direction;
◆ name all the items;
◆ match all items within a class to one another;
◆ request a missing item.

Although the experiment just described clearly demonstrated the efficiency of the equivalence-based instructional approach, the use of nonsense forms and words may actually obscure, rather than highlight, the tremendous effects of this procedure. Thus, the prior approach used is presented within a hypothetical example. Table 7.5 presents the instructional items in the hypothetical example.

By way of explanation:

◆ the A items are teacher-spoken directives (e.g., "Touch toy or fruit or clothes");
◆ the B, C, and D items were pictures;

Table 7.4 Items Used During the Potential Expansion of the Classes to Include Requesting

Potential Class	A-Item (spoken by the teacher)	B-Item	C-Item	D-Item	Name Item	Request Item
1	"cug"	▓	⇧	₪	Says "cug"	Request "cug"
2	"vek"	○	§	Ж	Says "vek"	Request "vek"
3	"zid"	◎	╪	Ю	Says "zid"	Request "zid"

Table 7.5 Instructional Items Used to Establish the Hypothetical Classes "Toy," "Fruit" and "Clothes"

Potential Class	A-Item (spoken by the teacher)	B-Items (picture)	C-Items (picture)	D-Items (picture)	E-Items (Name item)	F-Items (Request Item)
1	Teacher says "toy"	doll	blocks	puzzles	Child says "toy"	Child requests "toy"
2	Teacher says "fruit"	apple	banana	orange	Child says "fruit"	Child requests "fruit"
3	Teacher says "clothes"	shirt	pants	socks	Child says "clothes"	Child requests "clothes"

- the E items were the child naming each according to their potential class membership (e.g., toy, fruit and clothes);
- the F items were the child asking for items, using the class name (e.g., toy, fruit and clothes).

Thus, Table 7.6 presents a sequence of instruction and testing based on the experimental study previously presented.

As Table 7.6 details, across the three classes, a total of nine skills may be directly taught to establish the three classes (steps 1 and 4) and a total of 27 skills may emerge without instruction (grayed steps 2, 3, 5, 6 and 7). Note this hypothetical example does not include the sequence training and emergent requesting used in the original study. Regardless, this represents a taught-to-emergent ratio of relations of 1:3 (for every skill taught, another three emerge for free). Although this is only a hypothetical example, this is a common outcome in equivalence-based instruction.

In the two examples just presented, members of each category became related even though they were physically dissimilar (Sidman, 2009). Additionally, following teaching that resulted in the child naming an item, the child was then capable of selecting that item when the teacher provided spoken directions (Egan & Barnes-Holmes, 2009; Finn et al., 2012). Thus, it appears that because of the equivalence-based instructional protocols, a taught behavior (e.g., naming by the student) set the occasion for the child to respond to a teacher's stimulus (e.g., spoken direction), in the absence of any training. As stated above, Skinner (1957) defined each of the elementary verbal operants by describing what happens before and after that operant

Table 7.6 Hypothetical Instructional and Testing Sequence to Establish the Classes Toy, Fruit and Clothes

Step	Description	How?	Relations, Per class	Total Relations, for Three Classes
1	Teach naming of the B and C items	Taught	2	6
2	Test matching of B-to-C and C-to-B	Emergent	2	6
3	Test matching of B and C items to their spoken name, presented by the teacher (A-item)	Emergent	2	6
4	Teach matching of B-to-D	Taught	1	3
5	Test matching of D-to-B, C-to-D and D-C	Emergent	3	9
6	Test D naming	Emergent	1	3
7	Test matching of D items to their spoken name, presented by the teacher (A-item)	Emergent	1	3

(i.e., the context), so it is possible that a word learned under one set of conditions may not be observed under a different set of conditions (Egan & Barnes-Holmes, 2011; Lamarre & Holland, 1985; Twyman, 1996). This functional independence of each of the verbal operants is one of the elements that sets Skinner's analysis of human language apart from other, more traditional accounts (Petursdottir et al., 2005). For example, if a child with an autism spectrum disorder learns to name a berry, it is possible that this may not transfer to requesting berries. The fact that the two children in this study did just that (i.e., transferred their learning to a novel circumstance) speaks to the power of the equivalence instructional model. Given the challenges in language acquisition and development faced by youngsters diagnosed with autism spectrum disorders or other developmental disorders, we suggest that equivalence based instruction should be a fundamental tool in language instruction.

An important consideration when utilizing equivalence-based instruction to teach language skills is the complete evaluation of the child's language ability. Several studies have suggested that individuals who have language-based disabilities may be less likely to demonstrate these untaught relations and therefore fail to generalize these behaviors (Devany et al., 1986;

Eikeseth & Smith, 1992). This may be one reason why children with developmental disabilities may fail to acquire novel language from the natural environment, as neurotypical individuals do (Carr & Felce, 2000). Therefore, it is important to teach each of the different relations cited thus far (e.g, matching, naming, requesting) within the framework of equivalence-based instruction so as to increase the probability of more student skills than actually taught. Doing so may result in the quicker and more fluent acquisition of language for those children for whom language acquisition is challenging.

Another important note is that all of these procedures can be used with visual objects or stimuli, rather than just spoken or auditory. This, of course, is a skill fundamental to reading.

Summary

The procedures outlined within the chapter demonstrate how to design equivalence-based instruction to increase the acquisition of language plus the transfer of function (e.g., request, name, etc.) learned under one set of circumstances to another. While few studies have combined the theory of language outlined by Skinner (1957) with Sidman's stimulus equivalence model (cf., Sidman, 1994), it is critical to do so. Combining Skinner's theory of verbal behavior with equivalence-based instruction may accelerate the acquisition of sophisticated verbal behaviors and transfer of outcomes, especially for children with language-based disabilities. Similarly, understanding the generative nature of equivalence-based learning, compared to the steady but slower sequential learning of word relations under three-term contingencies, may help us understand the rapid acquisition of language for neurotypical children.

References

Carr, D., & Felce, D. (2000). Application of stimulus equivalence to language intervention for individuals with severe linguistic disabilities. *Journal of Intellectual and Developmental Disability, 25*(3), 181–205. https://doi.org/10.1080/13269780050144262

Devany, J. M., Hayes, S. C., & Nelson, R. O. (1986). Equivalence class formation in language-able and language-disabled children. *Journal of the Experimental Analysis of Behavior, 46*, 243–257. http://dx.doi.org/10.1901/jeab.1986.46-243

Egan, C. E., & Barnes-Holmes, D. (2009). Emergence of tacts following mand training in young children with autism. *Journal of Applied Behavior Analysis, 42*, 691–696. http://dx.doi.org/10.1901/jaba.2009.42-691

Egan, C. E., & Barnes-Holmes, D. (2011). Examining antecedent control over emergent mands and tacts in young children. *The Psychological Record, 61*, 127–140. http://dx.doi.org/10.1007/BF03395750

Eikeseth, S., & Smith, T. (1992). The development of functional and equivalence classes in high-functioning autistic children: The role of naming. *Journal of the Experimental Analysis of Behavior, 58*, 123–133. https://dx.doi.org/10.1901/jeab.1992.58-123

Finn, H. E., Miguel, C. F., & Ahearn, W. H. (2012). The emergence of untrained mands and tacts in children with autism. *Journal of Applied Behavior Analysis, 45*(2), 265–280. http://dx.doi.org/10.1901/jaba.2012.45-265

King, C. M. (2016). *A stimulus equivalence analysis of emergent mands, tacts, and listener behavior* (Unpublished doctoral dissertation). Simmons University.

Lamarre, J., & Holland, J. G. (1985). The functional independence of mands and tacts. *Journal of the Experimental Analysis of Behavior, 43*, 5–19. http://dx.doi.org/10.1901/jeab.1985.43-5

Petursdottir, A. I, Carr, J. E., & Michael, J. (2005). Emergence of mands and tacts of novel objects among preschool children. *The Analysis of Verbal Behavior, 21*, 59–74. http://dx.doi.org/10.1007/BF03393010

Sidman, M. (1994). *Equivalence relations and behavior: A research story*. Authors Cooperative Inc.

Sidman, M. (2009). Equivalence relations and behavior: An introductory tutorial. *The Analysis of Verbal Behavior, 25*, 5–17. http://dx.doi.org/10.1007/BF03393066

Skinner, B. F. (1957). *Verbal Behavior*. Appleton-Century-Crofts.

Twyman, J. (1996). The functional independence of impure mands and tacts of abstract stimulus properties. *The Analysis of Verbal Behavior, 13*, 1–19. http://dx.doi.org/10.1007/BF03392903

8

Teaching Science Content to Elementary Students via Equivalence-Based Instruction

Emily Leonard

Introduction

My name is Emily Leonard. I have a Ph.D. in Behavior Analysis from Simmons University. I am a doctoral-level BCBA and I have taught third-grade since 2009. My classroom includes a range of students with Individual Educational Plans (IEPs) and I draw on my behavioral background for both academic accommodations and behavioral supports. The following chapter describes my teaching of sophisticated science concepts to neurotypical students and students with special education challenges within the actual classroom.

General Method for All Experiments

The goal of all three studies was to efficiently and effectively teach children science classification skills within the classroom. All three studies used conditional discrimination training (matching-to-sample) and tested for the emergence of untaught science relations consistent with equivalence class and concept formation. The goal of these three studies was to teach students

DOI: 10.4324/9781003297161-8

science classification of Carnivore, Herbivore, and Omnivore using pictures and text. All the items were visual and formed three groups (A, B, and C). Each group in turn contained three items: Group A (*Carnivore, Herbivore, Omnivore*) and Group C (*Eats Meat, Eats Plants, Eats Both*), which were written words. Group B contained three pictures of skull profiles, corresponding to the classes Carnivore, Herbivore and Omnivore. Table 8.1 lists the items used in these studies.

The first experiment utilized this teaching technique as remedial instruction for a student with attention deficit hyperactivity disorder (ADHD), dyslexia, and an autism spectrum disorder (ASD). The student had failed to demonstrate mastery of relations between the printed names of animal types, printed descriptions of their diets and pictures of animal skulls through traditional science lessons. Experiments 2 and 3 replicated the results of Experiment 1, with neurotypical children within two different grades and classroom settings.

The physically dissimilar items appear in vertical columns of Table 8.1: Group A, Group B, and Group C. The three classes are depicted in the horizontal rows and include one item from each of the groups. Experiment 1 differed from the other two experiments in that the C3 text read "Eats Plants and Meat." In Experiments 2 and 3 it read "Eats Both." This change occurred to the C items to keep the word length of the descriptions similar.

On each trial, students selected their answers from an array of comparison items, as described in Chapters 2 and 4. Before training, each student completed a series of pretests to ensure they could do identity match-to-sample (match identical stimuli based upon physical characteristics, Chapter 2) and to determine if any of the concepts to be taught were already mastered.

In all sessions, each item in a group was presented as the sample six times and the presentations of comparisons and samples were randomized in such a manner that the presentation and position were unpredictable. Training sessions contained intermixed trials of the relations to be taught. For example, sessions teaching the A-B relations consisted of all three types: matching the

Table 8.1 Items Used in the Experiments

Class	Items A: Printed Words	Items B: Pictures	Items C: Printed Words
1	Carnivore	Skull of a Carnivore	Eats Meat
2	Herbivore	Skull of a Herbivore	Eats Plants
3	Omnivore	Skull of a Omnivore	Eats Both

pictures of the skulls of carnivores, herbivores and omnivores to their related printed names, C-A-R-N-I-V-O-R-E, H-E-R-B-I-V-O-R-E, and O-M-N-I-V-O-R-E, respectively. During other teaching sessions, A-B and A-C relations were presented together.

Responses were considered correct when the student selected the comparison that was a member of the same teacher-defined class as the sample and responses were considered incorrect when the comparison selected was from a different teacher-defined class than the sample. Students were required to reach 100% mastery in the training phase to move on to posttests. Training was repeated until mastery was reached.

Posttests repeated the pretest conditions for all concepts and no reinforcement was provided. No additional prompts were provided and an incorrect choice merely initiated the next trial.

Experiment 1

The participant, Nolan, was a nine-year-old boy in the third grade. He was diagnosed with ASD, dyslexia, and ADHD, for which he took stimulant medication. Nolan was selected for this study because his performance on a previous science test suggested that he did not understand the classification of carnivores, herbivores, and omnivores, nor the skulls that corresponded to each. However, he could read the words *Herbivore, Carnivore,* and *Omnivore* and other text. He had experience with a touch pad on a laptop and required no instruction regarding the use of a mouse. Note, Nolan had no prior experience with MTS instruction or using PowerPoint® in slideshow mode.

Training and testing sessions occurred in Nolan's classroom or at a small worktable in the hall just outside the classroom. Nolan completed all testing and training on an Apple® 13″ MacBook® using PowerPoint® presentation software (Microsoft® Powerpoint® for Macs, 2011). A training trial was a PowerPoint® slide, divided into four quadrants. The sample stimulus always appeared in the top left quadrant and was outlined by a red frame. The three comparison stimuli appeared in the other three quadrants and were outlined by blue frames. Data were recorded using paper and pencil by the teacher sitting behind the student.

Teaching. Nolan's training occurred in two phases. The first phase involved an errorless learning fading procedure (Ellis et al., 1978; Etzel & LeBlanc, 1979), and the second phase only provided reinforcement for correct responses. During both phases, clicking on the correct comparison produced a feedback slide that included an audio chime accompanied by the text *You're*

Right on the computer screen for three seconds. The stimulus display for the next trial then appeared. An incorrect response terminated the trial and immediately produced the display for the next trial.

Training with fading involved both text-to-picture (A-B) and text-to-text (A-C) relations (Figure 8.1). Trials for both the A-B and A-C relations were presented in the same session. Eighteen A-B trials were presented first, followed by 18 A-C trials. During fading, the sample and three comparisons were presented and the two incorrect comparisons faded and disappeared (Microsoft® Powerpoint® feature) over three seconds thus leaving only the sample and the correct comparison on the screen. Clicking on the correct comparison was reinforced by presentation of the feedback slide (e.g., correct slide plus the chime) whereas clicking anywhere outside of the stimulus resulted in initiation of the next trial. The criterion for advancing to the differential reinforcement phase was completing three consecutive sessions with 100% accuracy.

Training with differential reinforcement started with teaching A-B relations (18 trials per session). The mastery criterion was accuracy of 100% across three consecutive sessions. Nolan then selected a prize from the classroom prize jar, and differential reinforcement training for the A-C relations (18 trials per session) began. The criterion for A-C training was 100% accuracy across three consecutive sessions.

Four posttest sessions were presented in the following order: transitive relations (B-C & C-B), symmetrical relations (C-A & B-A), trained relations (A-B and A-C), and tests for reflexivity (A-A, B-B, & C-C). When all sessions were complete, Nolan selected a final prize from the classroom prize jar.

Results. During pretests, Nolan matched all the items to identical samples with 100% accuracy. However, his accuracy on matching tasks involving physically dissimilar items was consistently below 55.5% for all relations.

During the fading phase of training, Nolan's matching performances indicated he had learned all A-B (printed word name to picture) and A-C (printed word name to printed word description) relations. However, when training progressed to Phase 2 (differential reinforcement only) his accuracy on A-B trials decreased to his pretest levels (33%). His accuracy rapidly increased across the first three differential reinforcement sessions. Training the A-B relations to 100% mastery required six sessions, whereas Nolan required thirteen sessions to learn the A-C relations.

During posttests, Nolan's performance demonstrated a high degree of accuracy, greater than 94%, across all relations. Nolan's performance on all matching tasks during the posttests suggested that three classes of equivalent stimuli had formed.

Discussion. Experiment 1 was conducted in Nolan's general education classroom after he failed to master the science concepts (i.e., carnivore, herbivore, and omnivore) through general education instruction. The MTS training procedure in this study modified the presentation of the science content, and after teaching two sets of relations (A-B and A-C) with differential reinforcement, Nolan demonstrated the emergence of the symmetrical relations B-A and C-A, and the transitive relations B-C and C-B. The MTS procedure was effective in producing emergent relations required to demonstrate equivalence classes with academic content used in a typical third-grade science education.

It was surprising that Nolan made many errors on trials with the A-B and A-C relations following the training with the fading procedure. The decrease in Nolan's accuracy at the start of the differential reinforcement procedure, following the fading procedure, suggested that the fading procedure did not establish the intended relations between the different science items. However, it appeared that the differential reinforcement sessions did, eventually, result in the emergence of all relations. It also took Nolan twice as many training sessions (thirteen total) for A-C relations as it did A-B relations. It is possible that since A-B relations were trained immediately after the fading condition they were learned more rapidly. Therefore, in Experiments 2 and 3 the fading procedure was eliminated, and A-B and A-C training were always presented in one session.

Error patterns also highlighted irrelevant stimulus features (e.g., skull direction) in the photographs (B-items), and text length in stimulus C3 (*Eats Meat and Plants)* which was two words longer than the text for the C1 (*Eats Meat*) and C2 (*Eats Plants*) items. These issues were corrected in Experiments 2 and 3. Regardless of the errors that occurred during instruction, the results from Experiment 1 suggested that the MTS procedures provided a method for teaching aspects of general-education science curriculum.

Given these encouraging outcomes, Experiment 2 was designed to evaluate whether the procedures from Experiment 1 would establish the same equivalence classes in a small group format, instead of one-to-one and when used as primary instruction for the science content, instead of as a remedial tool.

Experiment 2

Six third-grade students participated in Experiment 2. All students received the general third-grade education available in their classrooms. The classroom teachers reported that all of the students demonstrated grade-level skills, except for Sam. Sam spoke only Russian at home and frequently needed teacher support with English vocabulary. Sam also received small-group reading support from a specialist because reading assessments indicated his reading was below grade level. None of the participants had prior experience using MTS for instruction or experience using Qualtric® (Qualtrics, 2014), a survey program.

All training and testing occurred within a third-grade classroom and were conducted on Apple® iMac® computers, placed on a table in the rear of the classroom. Two computers were available, thus allowing two participants to work simultaneously. The computers faced away from each other to ensure the one student could not view the screen of the other station. During most sessions, the classroom was full of students, engaged in other academic activities.

Students completed all testing and training on an iMac® desktop computer using the Internet survey program Qualtrics®. The questions presented were in the form of MTS tasks. Each MTS presentation of four items (trial) was displayed on a new screen.

The sample item always appeared above the comparisons on the left side of the screen. If the student clicked on the sample, nothing happened. The three comparison items appeared below the sample in a horizontal row. The students were verbally instructed to select a comparison by either clicking on the actual comparison (text or picture) from the array or by clicking on the selection circle below a comparison. The student then clicked the arrow button in the bottom left corner of the screen to advance to the next trial.

At the end of each session the program calculated the percentage of correct selections and displayed it on the screen. It also displayed which comparison the participant selected on each trial. The experimenter then scored each trial by hand to determine the percent correct for each stimulus class.

Experiment 2 eliminated the fading procedure and used only differential reinforcement for training. Correct answers received a green check and incorrect selections received a red X. Additionally, the mastery criterion was lowered to a single session with 100% accuracy.

Pretesting was conducted and each student's teaching was determined based on their pretest results.

Instruction. During instruction, differential reinforcement solely was provided for each answer. When each training session was completed, a screen appeared that thanked the student. Once the student reached 100% accuracy with the targeted teaching session(s), posttests occurred in the same format as the pretest.

Results. Posttests revealed that all six students were 100% accurate for identity relations (matching a comparison to an identical sample).

All six students learned the targeted relations quickly and with few errors. Five of the six students required only two training sessions and the remaining student, Suzanne, required four sessions to reach 100% accuracy. Consequently, all six participants demonstrated the emergent stimulus-to-stimulus relations indicating the formation of three different three-member equivalence classes.

The number of training sessions that each participant required in Experiment 2 was less than Nolan required in Experiment 1. This suggests that the procedural changes increased the effectiveness. Specifically, in delivering feedback for both correct answers (green checkmark) and incorrect answers (red X), the feedback was more specific. Additionally, in Experiment 2 students were able to click on multiple comparisons during a trial before submitting their final answer. It should be noted that Nolan and the students in Experiment 2 had different learning histories, where Nolan had already been exposed to the pictures and text during general-education science lessons, and therefore may have had a longer history of errors than the students from Experiment 2.

Other procedural changes were aimed at decreasing the amount of time required for training. The mastery criterion was reduced to a single session with 100% accuracy and the fading procedure used in Experiment 1 was eliminated. Each training session in Experiment 2 took students approximately six to eight minutes to complete. These two procedural changes were effective and increased the efficiency of the procedures.

During posttests, the performances of all six participants indicated equivalence-class formation. For all participants, accuracy was at 89% or higher for all stimulus-to-stimulus relations. This is particularly noteworthy for Suzanne, since she had the lowest levels of accuracy during pretesting and required the greatest number of training sessions. Suzanne's results suggest the extended number of training sessions due to errors did not negatively affect class formation.

The posttest results indicated that all six students formed the three equivalence classes, consisting of printed names, pictures and printed descriptions.

Based on the results of Experiment 1 and Experiment 2, Experiment 3 was designed to replicate these interventions with a younger general-education population of kindergarten students. The only experimental change made was to switch the device from the computer to an Apple® iPad®. This allowed younger students to select their answer by touching the items displayed on the screen and also allowed students to bring the Apple® iPad®

to their workstation. The use of the Apple® iPad® easily integrated into the regular classroom routine.

Experiment 3

Experiment 3 taught five kindergarten students the same science concepts using the same procedures from Experiment 2. In order to participate, students had to be highly accurate on pretests assessing students' ability to match comparisons to identical samples. The five kindergarten students in the study were all six-year-olds with high academic skills, according to their teachers. According to the school's reading assessment system, all five participants read beyond grade level. None of the participants had prior experience with MTS instruction, Apple® iPad® for instruction in the classroom setting, or experience with Qualtrics®. All five participants reported having used an Apple® iPad® at home to play games.

All sessions were conducted while the student was seated at a worktable in the classroom. During training sessions, other kindergarten students were in the same room participating in their regular classroom routine. The kindergarten students completed all testing and training on an Apple® iPad® using Qualtrics® surveys. Students were instructed to select a comparison by touching it.

Pretests were conducted across three sessions to decrease the time required for a student to complete a session. This allowed for easier integration into the kindergarten schedule. The posttest procedures were identical to the pretests.

Instruction. The number of training sessions for participants ranged from 4 to 14 sessions requiring 7 to 28 days. Whenever possible, posttests began on the same day the student met the mastery criteria.

All kindergarten students reached 100% accuracy within 4 to 14 teaching sessions. Kindergartners required a greater number of training sessions than third-graders. This supports results from previous studies that suggested that young children have difficulty acquiring arbitrary matching and that training may take longer (Pilgrim et al., 2000). Additionally, the accuracy of all kindergarteners was lower in pretesting, The amount of time third-graders and kindergarteners spent in each training session was about the same.

Posttests revealed that all five participants demonstrated all untaught relations between the science items, indicating the formation of three equivalence classes.

General Discussion

All three studies used equivalence-based instruction to teach children science concepts in the general education classroom. The MTS procedures were effective as a curriculum modification (Experiment 1) and as a primary instructional strategy (Experiment 2 and Experiment 3).

The participant in Experiment 1, Nolan, had several diagnosed learning disabilities, including autism, and required instructional modifications. The results from Experiment 1 suggested the procedures worked as a modification to academic instruction and resulted in the emergence of untrained relations, suggesting the formation of equivalence classes.

The results from Experiment 1 were socially significant (i.e., important to Nolan and not only the researcher and teacher). Nolan accessed modified instruction for the science curriculum within his general education classroom, and learned the relations among the pictures, labels, and additional text that demonstrated acquisition of the same science conceptual content as his peers. The training procedures, materials, and time required to complete training and testing sessions were flexible enough to be conducted without adjusting Nolan's typical schedule. Also, Nolan often asked for the opportunity to work on teaching sessions, which suggested that the MTS tasks on the computer were a preferred activity.

The purpose of Experiments 1, 2, and 3 was to demonstrate that equivalence-based instruction could be integrated into classroom instruction. Therefore, changes were made following Experiment 1 to increase the flexibility of the procedures. Computer-based instruction allowed for immediate feedback as students moved through the curriculum at their own paces (Skinner, 1968). The advantages of computerized instruction include requiring minimal teacher training and making it less likely that a teacher will unintentionally prompt or influence a student's response than with tabletop instruction. However, the use of PowerPoint® required the presence of a teacher. By switching from PowerPoint® to Qualtrics® in Experiments 2 and 3, feedback was delivered and data were collected for each response without requiring a teacher to be present. The automation increased the flexibility of the teaching method and allowed several students to participate simultaneously within the classroom while the teacher worked with other students.

Another change that increased the flexibility of the procedures was eliminating the fading procedure used in Experiment 1. The fading procedure did not decrease errors in the differential reinforcement phase and increased the amount of time required for training. In Experiments 2 and 3 the feedback was added for incorrect trials during training. The results from Experiments

2 and 3 suggested that the conditioned reinforcer of the green check mark appearing next to the correct response and conditioned punisher of the red X appearing next to the incorrect response were effective differential consequences. All participants, even the kindergarten students, mastered the trained relations, and demonstrated emergent symmetrical and transitive relations among items.

The final procedural change made was the elimination of back-up reinforcers (prizes) delivered for completing sessions. This is an important consideration in the classroom setting because it meant that participating students were not earning prizes that were not available to nonparticipating students. Removing back-up reinforcers also reduced additional resources needed in the classroom.

Experiments 2 and 3 extended existing research by demonstrating that the procedures used for pretesting, training, and posttests can be conducted within a general-education classroom environment. Additionally, the results showed that training can be conducted simultaneously for several students and that the time requirement for each session was brief. Training sessions of 36 trials typically took third-graders approximately six minutes, and kindergarteners eight minutes. The brevity of these sessions made it easy for students to complete MTS tasks at various points in their school day, and the teachers were able to continue to deliver instruction to other students. When possible, students were given the opportunity to complete multiple sessions. In the kindergarten classrooms, the sessions often fit naturally into working in stations that existed in the daily schedule.

The results from Experiments 1, 2, and 3 demonstrated that the equivalence-based instruction was effective and efficient. Students demonstrated a greater number of derived relations than the number of relations directly trained. For all students, nine relations were possible (i.e., A-A, B-B, C-C, A-B, B-A, A-C, C-A, B-C, and C-B) per class and, at most, only two relations were trained. These teaching procedures can be applied as a curriculum modification, as demonstrated in Experiment 1, or as a primary instructional method (Experiments 2 and 3). Concept formation, therefore, was taught economically, within the classroom, and decreased the amount of time special-education students spent separated from typical peers.

The equivalence-based instruction described in these three studies demonstrates a flexible and efficient teaching procedure. The instruction was used as both remediation and as primary instruction and successfully taught science concepts to young learners (six-year-olds) as well as a student with a diagnosed learning disability. The individualized training ensured each student achieved the criteria for mastery for sophisticated concepts and moved through the academic content at their own pace.

References

Ellis, W. D., Ludlow, B. L., & Walls, R. T. (1978). Learning, transfer, and retention of errorless fading versus trial-and-error teaching. *Psychological Reports, 43*, 553–554. https://doi.org/10.2466/pr0.1978.43.2.553

Etzel, B. C., & LeBlanc, J. M. (1979). The simplest treatment alternative: The law of parsimony applied to choosing appropriate instructional control and errorless-learning procedures for the difficult-to-teach child. *Journal of Autism and Developmental Disorders, 9*, 361–382. https://doi.org/10.1007/BF01531445

Microsoft® Powerpoint® for Macs (Version 14.3.1) [Software and presentation program]. (2011). Available from https://www.microsoft.com/

Pilgrim, C., Jackson, J., & Galizio, M. (2000). Acquisition of arbitrary conditional discriminations by young normally developing children. *Journal of the Experimental Analysis of Behavior, 73*, 177–193. https://doi.org/10.1901/jeab.2000.73-177

Qualtrics. (2014). Qualtrics: Online survey technology [Online surveys]. Unpublished instrument. https://doi.org/www.qualtrics.com/

Skinner, B. F. (1968). The science of learning and the art of teaching. In J. Vargas (Eds.), *Technology of teaching* (pp. 9–28). Appleton-Century-Crofts.

9

Design and Implementation of Equivalence-Based Instruction

Russell W. Maguire, Ronald F. Allen and Colleen Yorlets

As noted in Chapter 4, equivalence-based instruction can be conducted in a number of ways. Chapters 3 and 4 introduced sorting as a means for pretests and posttests for emergent relations, and Chapters 5 and 6 suggested alternative instruction protocols (e.g., the use of complex stimuli and differential outcomes, respectively) to improve the already effective equivalence-based protocol. This chapter presents one method to pretest, teach and posttest for academic relations. This is only one way to teach and test, although it is a fairly standard one. An outline of this sequence appears in Table 9.1.

Step 1: Preparation

    a   Selection of Items to Teach;
    b   Determination of the Mode of Instruction;
    c   Data Collection

Step 2: Pretesting

    a   Reflexivity;
    b   Relations to be Taught;

DOI: 10.4324/9781003297161-9

Table 9.1 An Outline to Conduct Equivalence-based Instruction

<u>**Step 1: Preparation:**</u>
a   Selection of Items to Teach;
b   Determination of the Mode of Instruction;
c   Data Collection.
<u>**Step 2: Pretesting:**</u>
a   Reflexivity;
b   Relations-to-be-Taught;
c   Symmetry;
d   Transitivity;
e   Data Collection;
f   Assessment.
<u>**Step 3: Instruction**</u>
a   Many-to-One Training Structure;
b   Errorless Instruction;
c   Use of Complex Stimuli;
d   Reinforcement;
e   Differential Outcomes;
f   Data Collection.
<u>**Step 4: Posttests:**</u>
a   Reflexivity;
b   Relations Taught;
c   Symmetry;
d   Transitivity;
e   Data Collection;
f   Assessment.

c   Symmetry;
d   Transitivity;
e   Data Collection;
f   Assessment.

Step 3: Instruction

a   Many-to-One Training Structure;
b   Errorless Instruction;
c   Use of Complex Stimuli;
d   Reinforcement;

e   Differential Outcomes;
f   Data Collection.

Step 4: Posttests

a   Reflexivity;
b   Relations Taught;
c   Symmetry;
d   Transitivity;
e   Data Collection;
f   Assessment.

The lesson that appears after this chapter follows this sequence.

Step 1: Preparation

Selection of Items to Teach

The teacher first must decide what items to teach to establish the targeted concept and how these items are to be represented. Those skills are best identified by the teachers and family in the student's life. The skills to teach may be determined by the teacher's experience and knowledge of the student and/or based on the family's feedback. Additionally, one may conduct formal assessments such as the VB-MAPPS (Verbal Behavior Milestones Assessment and Placement Program, Sundberg, 2008) and the ABBLS (The Assessment of Basic Language and Learning Skills, Partington & Sundberg, 1998; Partington, 2010). Finally, teaching targets may also be identified by the student's IEP (Individual Educational Plan).

Regardless, please recall that *at least* three concepts need be taught as the same time, with each consisting of *at least* three items. So, whatever the specific skills to be taught are, the teacher must make sure that there are three items for each class and that each item can be represented in trials. For example, some items, such as some verbs, are difficult to represent visually.

Table 9.2 may guide your selection. The numbers indicate the individual classes and the letters indicate the individual items within each class (this alphanumeric notation was described in Chapter 3 and appears throughout subsequent chapters. Each letter should refer to items that share a common form (e.g., spoken words, printed words, geometric forms, images of animals, etc.). For example:

- the letter A may refer to teacher directions (e.g., "Touch A1," "Touch A2," "Touch A3") with each number referring to a different spoken instruction (e.g., "Touch Apple," "Touch Banana," "Touch Grapes");
- the letter B may refer to pictures, with the numbers referring to different pictures, corresponding to the spoken instructions (e.g., B1 = a picture of an apple; B2 = a picture of a banana; B3 = a picture of grapes);
- the letter C may refer to printed words with the numbers referring to different printed words, corresponding to the spoken instructions and pictures (e.g., C1 = the printed word A-P-P-L-E; C2 = the printed word B-A-N-A-N-A; C3 = the printed word G-R-A-P-E-S).

Thus, the items that have different letter designations (e.g., A, B, or C) but the same number (e.g., 1, 2, or 3) are items targeted to be related and become members of the same class (e.g., A1, B1, C1 or A2, B2, C2 or A3, B3, C3).

The boxes in the upper portion of Table 9.2 may be used to plan instruction. The lower portion of Table 9.2 provides an example of items that may be used for the instruction of the classes "dog," "cat" and "gerbil." Of course, you may add columns and rows to increase the number of classes and items within each class or change the specific items within each class.

Table 9.2 Blank Planning Table for Equivalence-based Instruction

Items	Stimulus Classes		
	1	2	3
A B C			

Sample: Completed Planning Table for Equivalence-Based Instruction

Items	Stimulus Classes		
	1	2	3
A B C	"Dog" Picture of dog Printed word: D-O-G	"Cat" Picture of cat Printed word: C-A-T	"Gerbil" Picture of gerbil Printed word: G-E-R-B-I-L

Mode of Instruction

Next, the teacher must decide how to present the teaching and test trials: tabletop presentation or some type of electronic means. When making this decision, one should consider if there are modes of presentation best suited for the learner based on prerequisite skills, history, and preference.

Also, consider the teacher-to-learner ratio. For example, if instruction is to occur in a small-group setting then the students must possess certain levels of independence and skill. Leonard (Chapter 8) presented three experiments, two which conducted EBI in small groups (i.e., 5 or 6 students) with instructional materials presented on either a computer or iPad. However, this instructional style (i.e., small group via computers) should not be construed as a typical arrangement, as many students, including students with development and intellectual disabilities, may find such an approach challenging.

There are benefits and limitations to using tabletop and computer-based instruction. In tabletop instruction, no electronic device or technology skills are required. Depending on the presentation format, however, an instructor may need to physically present materials and reinforcers and score data for each trial. This may prove difficult given all the other demands that impinge on teachers' time. On the other hand, computer-based instruction may perform these tasks automatically, but one must consider the time and complexity required to program the relevant software and to train the teacher and student to use it. Additionally, technology may not always be available, can malfunction, and may not be feasible for all academic topics. All that being said, both tabletop and computer-based instruction can be effective, so teachers and learners are not limited if they use one as opposed to another.

Data Collection

In order to evaluate the effectiveness of the procedures used, specific data must be collected (not just a "+" versus "−" to represent correct versus incorrect responses). The data sheet being used, therefore, is important and can be used to facilitate accurate trial presentation, response scoring, the unique reinforcers used as well as data analysis (e.g., what item was selected when a specific item was the sample).

It is suggested using a data sheet similar to the one displayed in Table 6.4 (Chapter 6). This data sheet specifies not only the items to be matched to one another but also the unique reinforcers to be delivered for correct responding for each trial. Also, as noted in Chapter 4, the use of such predetermined data sheets details the exact trial sequence of the teaching session, including the position of comparison items and the presentation of sample items. Given this setup, the teacher can merely circle the student's answer, instead of noting a correct versus an incorrect answer. This allows the teacher to conduct a trial-by-trial error analysis to determine if any bias influenced student answers (e.g., position or item or reinforcer preferences, Dickson et al., 2006).

Step 2: Pretesting

It is recommended that pretests and posttests be conducted via the sorting procedure described in Chapter 3. As noted in Chapter 3, MTS pretests and posttests can be time- and labor-intensive, for both the teacher and the student (Arntzen et al., 2015; Critchfield, 2018; Palmer et al., 2020). Also, because these tests must be conducted in the absence of feedback, student responses may not be accurate. Thus, under these conditions, sorting tests may produce more reliable outcomes as compared to MTS tests.

Sorting tests should be conducted before and after teaching. Table 9.3 presents a sequence of sorting pretests assessing reflexivity, symmetry, transitivity and the relations to be taught. The left column lists the pretests to be conducted, in sequence. The comparisons change from test to test and consist of 18 randomly shuffled cards representing 6 cards each for each of three items (i.e., A1, A2, A3 or B1, B2, B3 or C1, C2, C3). The right three columns represent "boxes" with one card placed on the table, in front of each box, as the sample, face-up. The student is then given the 18 shuffled cards to sort into the boxes (match to the sample cards in the boxes). Note that depending on the test, the card in front of each box, serving as a sample, and the shuffled deck of cards will change, based on what is being assessed. This is described below.

Reflexivity

As previously reported in Chapters 1 and 2, reflexivity is the property of stimulus equivalence that assesses one's ability to match items based on physical identity. The first three pretests in Table 9.3 (numbers 1–3) details the different tests needed to assess matching different items based on physical identity. For example, if items are pictures, then an example of each picture is placed in front of each box and the student is to place replicas into the corresponding boxes, based on physical similarity.

Different pretests are conducted to assess the different forms of each class member (e.g., symbols, printed words, forms, etc.). Using the example in the lower portion of Table 9.2, if the goal of a pretest (or posttest, for that matter) is to assess the student's sorting pictures of dogs, cats and gerbils, based on an identical sample, then a picture of a dog would appear in front of one box, the picture of a cat would appear in front of another box and a picture of a gerbil would appear in front of the final box. The student would be given a shuffled deck of 18 cards to sort into the boxes: 6 pictures of a dog, 6 pictures of a cat and 6 pictures of a gerbil.

As noted in previous chapters, one cannot assess reflexivity with spoken names as it is difficult, although not impossible, to present identical comparisons simultaneously (Dube et al., 1993).

Relations to Be Taught

Once the teacher has decided the relations to teach, they must be pretested, to ensure that they need to be taught. Table 9.3 lists these pretests (numbers 4 and 6), assuming a one-to-many teaching approach: matching B items to A and then to C items. These pretests place the sample of the to-be-taught relations in front of the boxes, and the comparisons of the to-be-taught relations form a pile of 18 cards to be sorted in the boxes, matched to the samples.

This approach works best if the samples (e.g., the cards placed in front of the boxes) are visual or three-dimensional (physical items). However, even if the sample is an auditory item (e.g., "Touch _____") this approach can still be applied. Using the example in the lower portion of Table 9.2, suppose the relation to be taught is matching pictures of animals to their spoken name (relation A-B). The teacher gives the student a shuffled deck of 18 cards to sort into the boxes, consisting of 6 pictures of a dog, 6 pictures of a cat and 6 pictures of a gerbil. Then the teacher may say something like "Put the dogs in this box, cats in this box and gerbils in this box," while pointing to the relevant boxes. This instruction may be repeated as often as necessary throughout the test. Additionally, this process may be enhanced via employ technology. AbleNet, Inc. (AbleNet, Inc., 2022) is a company that makes push-button switches that can record teacher statements, which can then be played back when the student pushes the button. Thus, a switch could be placed in front of a box with the name of the sample prerecorded. The student would push the button to hear the sample and then sort the relevant cards. Finally, the same may be done on computers using a software program, such as PowerPoint.

Symmetry

Symmetry is another property of equivalence. Once a relation has been taught, symmetry is demonstrated if the reverse of that relation is performed in the absence of any training (i.e., the original comparison is now the sample and the original sample is now the comparison). Since the recommended method of testing is the simple-to-complex protocol (Chapter 4), symmetry of the relations to be taught are to be assessed following each specific relation-to-be taught pretest. As a result, following the pretest for the A-B relation (relation to be taught, #4) the pretest for B-A (symmetry, #5) occurs, and following the pretest for the C-B relation (relation to be taught, #6) the pretest for B-A (symmetry, #7) occurs.

As with other tests, assessing the symmetrical relation to one that involves an auditory sample is difficult, although not impossible (Dube et al., 1993). If the relation to be taught involves a spoken-word sample then the symmetrical relation must involve spoken-word comparisons. It is impossible to present spoken-word comparisons simultaneously, as one would do with visual comparisons. In these cases, one does not need to conduct tests for symmetry but instead conduct the combined tests of symmetry and transitivity (Sidman & Tailby, 1982). In these cases, if transitivity emerges (see below for tests of transitivity), then one may assume that symmetry is demonstrated. An example may prove illustrative, using the example in Table 9.2. Assume the student is taught to select the picture of a dog (B1) and the printed word D-O-G (C1) when the teacher says, "Touch dog" (A1). Thus, the two relations to be taught can be described as A1-B1 and A1-C1. Testing for symmetry between B1-A1 and C1-A1 would be difficult because the spoken-word samples "dog," "cat" and "gerbil" cannot be present simultaneously as comparisons. However, in this case, if transitivity emerges then symmetry must be present. Why this occurs is beyond the scope of this book, but for the reader who wishes to explore this issue further, she is directed to Sidman and Tailby (1982) and Sidman (1994).

Transitivity

The third property of equivalence is transitivity. Transitivity occurs when relations between items develop that have not been directly related to one another but have been related to a common third element. These new relations must occur in the absence of instruction. For example, if one teaches the A-B and C-B relations, with the B-item serving as the common element (a node, Fields et al., 1984) then if the A-C and C-A relations emerge, without direct teaching, transitivity has been demonstrated. Pretests numbers 8 and 9 assess for transitivity.

It is suggested that each of the pretests be administered at least three times, to rule out the potential for false results. Also, sorting should be conducted in the absence of any feedback, although reinforcement could be provided for other, unrelated behaviors such as paying attention and on-task behavior to facilitate continued student responding.

It is important to note that these sorting procedures are different from the typical sorting protocol, cited in the literature. In the typical sorting protocol, the student is given a pile of cards containing replicas of all the items from all the classes and the goal is to group the ones together that are related, in some manner. Because all the class items are presented together, the student may erroneously group items according to criteria different from what the teacher may have intended (e.g., put all the pictures together instead of matching corresponding printed words to relevant pictures). The sorting procedure

Table 9.3 Sample Sorting Pretest Sequence

Samples (in front of each box)			
Reflexivity Pretest #1	**Box #1**	**Box #2**	**Box #3**
Comparisons: 18 cards (6 each of A1, A2, A3 randomly shuffled)	Item A1	Item A2	Item A3
Reflexivity Pretest #2 **Comparisons**: 18 cards (6 each of B1, B2, B3 randomly shuffled)	**Box #1** Item B1	**Box #2** Item B2	**Box #3** Item B3
Reflexivity Pretest #3 **Comparisons**: 18 cards (6 each of C1, C2, C3 randomly shuffled)	**Box #1** Item C1	**Box #2** Item C2	**Box #3** Item C3
Relation to Be Taught: A-B Pretest #4 **Comparisons**: 18 cards (6 each of B1, B2, B3 randomly shuffled)	**Box #1** Item A1	**Box #2** Item A2	**Box #3** Item A3
Symmetry: B-A Pretest #5 **Comparisons**: 18 cards (6 each of A1, A2, A3 randomly shuffled)	**Box #1** Item B1	**Box #2** Item B2	**Box #3** Item B3
Relation to Be Taught: C-B Pretest #6 **Comparisons**: 18 cards (6 each of B1, B2, B3 randomly shuffled)	**Box #1** Item C1	**Box #2** Item C2	**Box #3** Item C3
Symmetry: B-C Pretest #7 **Comparisons**: 18 cards (6 each of C1, C2, C3 randomly shuffled)	**Box #1** Item B1	**Box #2** Item B2	**Box #3** Item B3
Transitivity: A-C Pretest #8 **Comparisons**: 18 cards (6 each of C1, C2, C3 randomly shuffled)	**Box #1** Item A1	**Box #2** Item A2	**Box #3** Item B3
Transitivity: C-A Pretest #9 **Comparisons**: 18 cards (6 each of A1, A2, A3 randomly shuffled)	**Box #1** Item C1	**Box #2** Item C2	**Box #3** Item C3

presented here avoids this dilemma as the sample card and comparison cards to be sorted are restricted to the specific relation being assessed. For example, pretests #1 and #4 both use the items A1, A2 and A3 as sample cards but pretest #1 uses only items A1, A2 and A3 as comparisons, to be sorted, whereas pretest #4 uses items B1, B2 and B3 as comparisons, to be sorted. Thus, this sorting procedure assesses specific relations, similar to DTT/MTS, but requires far less effort and time, for the teacher and student, as compared to DTT/MTS.

Data Collection

Data collection for sorting pretests and posttests can initially be a photograph of the completed sort as permanent product data collection (Cooper et al.,

Many-to-One

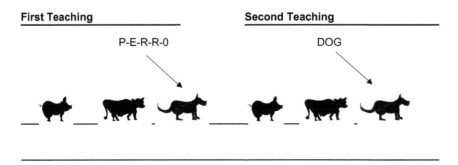

Figure 9.1 Example of the Many-to-One Training Method

2020). These data can then be transferred to a data sheet to document student responding.

Assessment

The teacher needs to identify the level of accuracy indicating that the student "knows" the relation between items. Given the recommendation that each relation be assessed on at least six occasions within each pretest, it is suggested that the acquisition criterion be at least five out of six correct matches (e.g., according to the teacher-defined classes) for each relation. Of course, this level of accuracy must be consistent across the three pretests for that performance. Relations between items that are below this level should be considered targets for teaching, whereas relations between items that are at or above this level should be considered known and do not require instruction.

Step 3: Instruction

Many-to-One Training

As noted in Chapter 4, it is recommended that teaching to form concepts or classes should be conducted via the many-to-one method. Figure 9.1 provides an example of this type of training. Note that in this example the comparison remains unchanged across the two different teachings (e.g., the picture of the dog is the comparison) but the samples change based on the relation assessed. Thus, in the first teaching the student is taught to match pictures to the Spanish printed words and in the second teaching the student is taught to match the very same pictures to the English printed words.

Errorless Instruction

The occurrence of errors during instruction may interfere with skill acquisition and the formation of classes (Green, 2001; Lancioni & Smeets, 1986; MacDuff et al., 2001). It is recommended that instruction occur using an errorless procedure, such as delayed prompt (Touchette & Howard, 1984), superimposition and fading (Birkan et al., 2007), or stimulus fading (De Graff et al., 2007). Regardless of the procedure used, the goal is to limit errors and increase the probability that untrained relations will emerge and classes will form (Chapter 5).

Use of Complex Stimuli

If appropriate, items can be combined, such as a picture and its related printed word, in one comparison. This decreases the number of relations needed to be taught and might accelerate the emergence of untrained relations. Additionally, given that the environment is full of naturally-occurring complex items, incorporating such elements into instruction may help to facilitate generalization to real-world settings.

Reinforcement

It is important that during instruction one employs a documented reinforcer (i.e., one that has been shown to increase the behavior for a given student, Cooper et al., 2020). To ensure that the reinforcers used during teaching are effective, one should conduct a preference or a reinforcer assessment prior to teaching (Dube et al., 1987; Dube et al.,1989; Chong & Carr, 2010; Fisher et al., 1996; Fisher et al., 1992).

Differential Outcomes

Differential outcomes has been defined as the application of a unique reinforcer for each skill being taught (Mok et al., 2010). The application of differential outcomes during equivalence-based instruction may take the form of restricting a specific reinforcer to each potential class: the relations taught within each class would use a reinforcer specific to those relations. Figure 6.1 in Chapter 6 provides a data sheet with differential outcomes. As the reader can see, each reinforcer used is assigned, and restricted to, a specific class of items. The benefit of differential outcomes may be that the relations to be taught may be acquired quicker, and the probability of their respective classes forming may increase.

If one uses differential outcomes during instruction then one must ensure that all reinforcers are of comparable quality and effectiveness. This is another reason why preference and/or reinforcer assessments should be conducted prior to instruction so that a number of equally effective reinforcers are used.

Instructional-Material Presentation

It is important that the items used during instruction are presented in a balanced manner and appear as comparisons and samples an equal number of times, in all positions (Figures 4.4 and 4.5, Chapter 4). Teachers may replace the items in these data sheets with the academic items relevant to the student being taught. Using a preplanned data sheet details the trial-by-trial sequence of teaching sessions, as well as the placement of all comparisons and samples. They also aid in data collection, in that the teacher merely circles the student response. Finally, preplanning the teaching session results in the session running smoothly and quickly.

Step 4: Posttest

Posttests should be conducted similarly to pretests, previously described in this chapter. In fact, the same outline presented in Table 9.2 should be used to conduct posttests. It is recommended that, during posttests, all relations, even those which may have been demonstrated during pretesting, be conducted. Conducting posttests for all relations allows confirmation of previously demonstrated relations as well as the newly trained and emergent relations. If relations are not initially demonstrated, posttests may be conducted again. As noted in Chapter 4, on occasion, the delayed emergence of critical relations may occur (Sidman, 1994) and additional testing may be required for relations to emerge.

As data are collected during pretests and posttests, data should be summarized in a tabular or graphic format to facilitate data analysis. Table 9.4 provides an example of a tabular summary. For each relation tested, the pretest and posttest data are recorded. A similar format could be used to summarize training data as well.

Figure 9.2 provides an example of a format for summarizing pretest and posttest data in graphic form. In this figure, the same data are summarized as in Table 9.4. Teachers may select the format they prefer.

Table 9.4 Tabular Summary of Testing Data

Tests				Relations					
	A-A	B-B	C-C	A-C	C-A	B-C	C-B	A-B	B-A
Pretest	83%	100%	83%	33%	0%	50%	16%	0%	0%
Posttest	100%	100%	100%	100%	100%	83%	100%	83%	100%

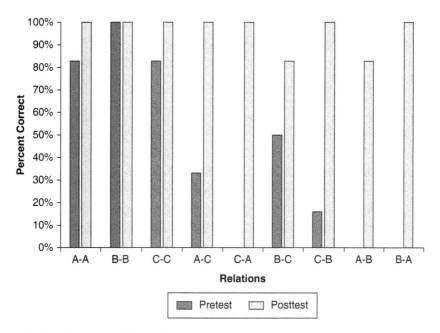

Figure 9.2 Graphic Summary of Testing Data

Conclusion

Sidman (1994) stressed the importance of implementing equivalence-based instruction within the classroom setting. He also recognized, however, that for this to occur, teachers need to be provided with adequate tools and training (Sidman, 1994). Realizing that a number of adaptations may need to occur so that the technology could be used within the natural environment, he still considered this an achievable goal (Sidman, 1994). It is hoped that this book helps to advance this goal by providing clear, practical, proven techniques for use in applied settings.

References

AbleNet, Inc. (2022). https://doi.org/www.ablenetinc.com

Arntzen, E., Norbom, A., & Fields, L. (2015). Sorting: An alternative measure of class formation. *Psychological Record*, *65*, 615–623. https://doi.org/10.1007/S40732-015-0132-5

Birkan, B., McClannahan, L. E., & Krantz, P. J. (2007). Effects of superimposition and background fading on the sight-word reading of a boy with autism. *Research in Autism Spectrum Disorders, 1*(2), 117–125. https://doi.org/10.1016/j.rasd.2006.08.003

Chong, I. M., & Carr, J. E. (2010). Failure to demonstrate the differential outcomes effect in children with autism. *Behavioral Interventions, 25,* 339–348. https://doi.org/10.1002/bin.318

Cooper, J. O., Heron, T. E., & Heward, W. L. (2020). *Applied behavior analysis* (3rd ed.). Pearson.

Critchfield, T. S. (2018). Efficiency is everything: Promoting efficient practice by harnessing derived stimulus relations. *Behavior Analysis in Practice, 11,* 206–210. https://doi.org/10.1007/s40617-018-0262-8

De Graff, S., Verhoeven, L., Bosman, A. M. T., & Hasselman, F. (2007). Integrated pictorial mnemonics and SF: Teaching kindergartners letter sounds. *British Journal of Educational Psychology, 77,* 519–539.

Dickson, C. A., Deutsch, C. K., Wang, S. S., Dube, W. V., & MacLean, W. E. (2006). Matching-to-sample assessment of stimulus overselectivity in students with intellectual Disabilities. *American Journal of Mental Retardation, 111,* 447–453. https://doi.org/10.1352/0895-8017(2006)111[447:MAOSOI]2.0.CO;2

Dube, W. V., Green, G., & Serna, R. W. (1993). Auditory successive conditional discrimination and auditory stimulus equivalence classes. *Journal of the Experimental Analysis of Behavior, 59,* 103–114. https://doi.org/10.1901/jeab.1993.59-103

Dube, W. V., McIlvane, W. J., Mackay, H. A., & Stoddard, L. T. (1987). Stimulus class membership established via stimulus-reinforcer relations. *Journal of the Experimental Analysis of Behavior, 47,* 159–175. https://doi.org/10.1901/jeab.1987.47-159

Dube, W. V., McIlvane, W. J., Maguire, R. W., Mackay, H. A., & Stoddard, L. T. (1989). Stimulus class formation and stimulus-reinforcer relations. *Journal of the Experimental Analysis of Behavior, 51,* 65–76.

Fields, L., Verhave, T., & Fath, S. (1984). Stimulus equivalence and transitive associations: A methodological analysis. *Journal of the Experimental Analysis of Behavior, 42,* 143–157. https://doi.org/10.1901/jeab.1984.42-143

Fisher, W. W., Piazza, C., Bowman, L. G., & Amari, A. (1996). Integrating caregiver report with a systematic choice assessment to enhance reinforcer identification. *American Journal on Mental Retardation, 101,* 15–25.

Fisher, W. W., Piazza, C. C., Bowman, L. G., Hagopian, L. P., Owens, J. C., & Slevin, I. (1992). A comparison of two approaches for identifying reinforcers for persons with severe and profound disabilities. *Journal of Applied Behavior Analysis, 25,* 491–498. https://doi.org/10.1901/jaba.1992.25-491

Green, G. (2001). Behavior analytic instruction for learners with autism: Advances in stimulus control technology. *Focus on Autism and Other Developmental Disabilities*, *16*, 72–85. https://doi.org/10.1177/10883576010 1600203

Lancioni, G. E., & Smeets, P. M. (1986). Procedures and parameters of errorless discrimination training with developmentally impaired individuals. In N. R. Ellis & N. W. Bray (Eds.), *International review of research in mental retardation* (pp. 135–164). Academic Press.

MacDuff, G. S., Krantz, P. J., & McClannahan, L. E. (2001). Prompts and prompt-fading strategies for people with autism. In C. Maurice, G. Green, & R. M. Foxx (Eds.), *Making a difference: Behavior intervention for autism*. PRO-ED.

Mok, L. W., Estévez, A. F., & Overmier, J. B. (2010). Unique outcome expectations as a training and pedagogical tool. *The Psychological Record*, *60*, 227–248. https://doi.org/10.1007/BF03395705

Palmer, S. K., Maguire, R. W., Lionello-DeNolf, K., & Braga-Kenyon, P. (2020). The inclusion of prompts in equivalence classes. *Journal of the Experimental Analysis of Behavior*, *115*(1), 255–271. https://doi.org/10.1002/jeab.655

Partington, J. W. (2010). *The assessment of basic language and learning skills-revised*. Behavior Analysts.

Partington, J. W., & Sundberg, M. L. (1998). *The assessment of basic language and learning skills*. Behavior Analysts.

Sidman, M. (1994). *Equivalence relations and behavior: A research story*. Authors Cooperative, Inc.

Sidman, M., & Tailby, W. (1982). Conditional discrimination vs. matching to sample: An expansion of the testing paradigm. *Journal of the Experimental Analysis of Behavior*, *37*, 5–22.

Sundberg, M. L. (2008). *VB-MAPP verbal behavior milestones assessment and placement program: A language and social skills assessment program for children with autism or other developmental disabilities*. Guide, AVB Press.

Touchette, P. E., & Howard, J. S. (1984). Errorless learning: Reinforcement contingencies and stimulus control transfer in delayed prompting. *Journal of Applied Behavior Analysis*, *17*, 175–188. https://doi.org/10.1901/jaba.1984.17-175

Appendix
Lesson Plan to Use Equivalence-Based Instruction

The purpose of this lesson plan is to provide the reader with an outline such that one may conduct an actual EBI program of their own choosing. The sequence and steps reported here were replicated from steps listed in Table 9.1 from Chapter 9.

Step 1: Preparation

The teacher must determine the following:

a   What to teach: It is assumed that the teacher has already established this.

b   Mode of instruction: It is assumed that the teacher has already detemined this.

c   Data collection: It is assumed that the mode of instruction will determine this. Regardless, data sheets and data summaries follow each step of this lesson plan.

The remainder of this lesson plan assumes that pretesting, teaching and conducting posttests will be done via paper and pencil, on tabletop, although this plan could be easily adapted to a computer program.

It is hoped that the following table will help organize the items to be used during EBI. The upper case letters identify the different forms of the items (e.g., auditory, visual, tactile, etc.), different yet related words (e.g., synomymns, antonyms, etc.) or the same word, in different languages. The numbers refer to the different classes to be formed.

Throughout, the reader can replace the alphanumerics that appear in the data sheets with the actual items they plan to use to conduct an EBI program. The following table should help with this process.

Blank Planning Table for Equivalence-Based Instruction

Items	Stimulus Classes		
	1	**2**	**3**
A			
B			
C			

Step 2: Pretesting

a. Reflexivity

Sorting "A" cards into boxes based on an identical "A" sample card, placed in front of the box.	**Sample** (place on the table in front of the box) **Comparisons**	**Box to Sort A1 Items Into**	**Box to Sort A2 Items Into**	**Box to Sort A3 Items Into**
		A1	**A2**	**A3**
		18 randomly shuffled cards consisting on 6 A1 items, 6 A2 items and 6 A3 items		

Sorting "B" cards into boxes based on an identical "B" sample card, placed in front of the box.	**Sample** (place on the table in front of the box) **Comparisons**	**Box to Sort B1 Items Into**	**Box to Sort B2 Items Into**	**Box to Sort B3 Items Into**
		B1	**B2**	**B3**
		18 randomly shuffled cards consisting on 6 B1 items, 6 B2 items and 6 B3 items		

Sorting "C" cards into boxes based on an identical "C" sample card, placed in front of the box.	**Sample** (place on the table in front of the box) **Comparisons**	**Box to Sort C1 Items Into**	**Box to Sort C2 Items Into**	**Box to Sort C3 Items Into**
		C1	**C2**	**C3**
		18 randomly shuffled cards consisting on 6 A1 items, 6 A2 items and 6 A3 items		

Note: No feedback regarding student sorting, correct or incorrect.
Note: Take a photograph of the grouped cards and then transfer this info to the data sheet that appears at the end of each test or teaching session.
Note: Conduct this pretest at least three times.

Data Collection for Reflexivity

Directions

Make a slash mark under the comparison item each time it appeared in the box when a specific item appeared as the sample (in front of the box). Complete one of these tables for each pretest conducted.

Comparisons									
Samples	**A1**	**A2**	**A3**	**B1**	**B2**	**B3**	**C1**	**C2**	**C3**
A1									
A2									
A3									
B1									
B2									
B3									
C1									
C2									
C3									

Step 2: Pretesting

b. Relations to Be Taught

Assuming a Many-to-One Method: Teach relations A-B and C-B

Sorting "B" cards into boxes based on an "A" sample card, placed in front of the box.	Sample (place on the table in front of the box) Comparisons	Box to Sort B1 Items Into	Box to Sort B2 Items Into	Box to Sort B3 Items Into
		A1	A2	A3
		18 randomly shuffled cards consisting of 6 B1 items, 6 B2 items and 6 B3 items		

Sorting "B" cards into boxes based on a "C" sample card, placed in front of the box.	Sample (place on the table in front of the box)	Box to Sort B1 Items Into	Box to Sort B2 Items Into	Box to Sort B3 Items Into
		C1	C2	C3
	Comparisons	18 randomly shuffled cards consisting of 6 C1 items, 6 C2 items and 6 C3 items		

Notes: No feedback regarding student sorting, correct or incorrect.
Take a photograph of the grouped cards and then transfer this info to the data sheet that appears at the end of each test or teaching session.
Conduct this pretest at least three times.

Data Collection for Relations to Be Taught

Directions

Make a slash mark under the comparison item each time it appeared in the box when a specific item appeared as the sample (in front of the box). Complete a table for each pretest conducted.

A-B Relation to Be Taught

	Comparisons		
	B1	**B2**	**B3**
A1			
A2			
A3			

C-B Relation-to-be-Taught

	Comparisons		
Samples	**B1**	**B2**	**B3**
C1			
C2			
C3			

Step 2: Pretesting

c. Symmetry

Assuming a Many-to-One Method: If relations A-B and C-B are taught, then **symmetry would be testing B-A and B-C**, respectively.

Sorting "A" cards into boxes based on a "B" sample card, placed in front of the box.	Sample (place on the table in front of the box)	Box to Sort A1 Items Into	Box to Sort A2 Items Into	Box to Sort A3 Items Into
		B1	B2	B3
	Comparisons	18 randomly shuffled cards consisting of 6 B1 items, 6 B2 items and 6 B3 items		

Sorting "C" cards into boxes based on a "B" sample card, placed in front of the box.	Sample (place on the table in front of the box)	Box to Sort C1 Items Into	Box to Sort C2 Items Into	Box to Sort C3 Items Into
		B1	B2	B3
	Comparisons	18 randomly shuffled cards consisting of 6 C1 items, 6 C2 items and 6 C3 items		

Note: No feedback regarding student sorting, correct or incorrect.
Note: Take a photograph of the grouped cards and then transfer this info to the data sheet that appears at the end of each test or teaching session.
Note: Conduct this pretest at least three times.

Data Collection for Symmetry

Directions

Make a slash mark under the comparison item each time it appeared in the box when a specific item appeared as the sample (in front of the box). Complete a table for each pretest conducted.

B-A Relation to Be Taught

	Comparisons		
Samples	**A1**	**A2**	**A3**
B1			
B2			
B3			

B-C Relation to Be Taught

	Comparisons		
Samples	**C1**	**C2**	**C3**
B1			
B2			
B3			

Step 2: Pretesting

d. Transitivity

Assuming a Many-to-One Method: if A-B and C-B, then symmetry would be B-A and B-C, respectively, thus **transitivity would be A-C and C-A**

Sorting "A" cards into boxes based on a "C" sample card, placed in front of the box.	Sample (place on the table in front of the box) Comparisons	Box to Sort A1 Items Into	Box to Sort A2 Items Into	Box to Sort A3 Items Into
		C1	C2	C3
		18 randomly shuffled cards consisting of 6 B1 items, 6 B2 items and 6 B3 items		

Sorting "C" cards into boxes based on an "A" sample card, placed in front of the box.	Sample (place on the table in front of the box) Comparisons	Box to Sort C1 Items Into	Box to Sort C2 Items Into	Box to Sort C3 Items Into
		A1	A2	A3
		18 randomly shuffled cards consisting of 6 C1 items, 6 C2 items and 6 C3 items		

Note: No feedback regarding student sorting, correct or incorrect.
Note: Take a photograph of the grouped cards and then transfer this info to the data sheet that appears at the end of each test or teaching session.
Note: Conduct this pretest at least three times.

Data Collection for Transitivity

Directions

Make a slash mark under the comparison item each time it appeared in the box when a specific item appeared as the sample (in front of the box). Complete a table for each pretest conducted.

A-C Relation

Samples	Comparisons		
	C1	C2	C3
A1			
A2			
A3			

C-A Relation

Samples	Comparisons		
	A1	A2	A3
C1			
C2			
C3			

Step 3: Instruction

a. Many-to-One Training Structure with Differential Outcomes

Directions

The following two data sheets are to be used for the A-B and the C-B teaching sessions. Note that the samples and comparisons are represented by the alphanumeric labels, previously discussed. The reader can replace these items with the names of the actual items to be taught via the find-and-replace function.

New alphanumerics appear in the forms of R1, R2 and R3. These represent different but comparable reinforcers to be used **exclusively** with the relations from class 1, class 2 and class 3, respectively. So, correct responding on the relations:

- ◆ A1-B1 and C1-B1 are followed by the R1 reinforcer:
- ◆ A2-B2 and C2-B2 are followed by the R2 reinforcer:
- ◆ A3-B3 and C3-B3 are followed by the R3 reinforcer.

The reader can replace these items with the names of the actual reinforcers to be used via the find-and-replace function.

Data Collection: Data Sheets

			LEFT	MIDDLE	RIGHT	Differential
A-B MATCHING-TO-SAMPLE DATA (MTS) SHEET						
The letters represent three different relations being taught. In this case matching B1, B2 and B3 comparisons to A1, A2, A3 samples, respectively.						
The designators (LEFT, MIDDLE, RIGHT) indicate the positions of the choices, from the learner's perspective. The shaded boxes indicate a correct choice.						
			LEFT	MIDDLE	RIGHT	Differential
	SAMPLE		COMPARISONS			Reinforcer
1	A1		B3	B2	B1	R1
2	A2		B1	B2	B3	R2
3	A3		B3	B1	B2	R3
4	A2		B3	B2	B1	R2
5	A1		B2	B3	B1	R1
6	A2		B2	B1	B3	R2
7	A3		B1	B3	B2	R3
8	A2		B2	B3	B1	R2
9	A3		B1	B2	B3	R3
10	A1		B2	B1	B3	R1
11	A2		B3	B1	B2	R2
12	A1		B1	B2	B3	R1
13	A3		B2	B1	B3	R3
14	A1		B1	B3	B2	R1
15	A3		B2	B3	B1	R3
16	A2		B1	B3	B2	R2
17	A1		B3	B1	B2	R1
18	A3		B3	B2	B1	R3

C-B MATCHING-TO-SAMPLE DATA (MTS) SHEET

The letters represent three different relations being taught. In this case matching B1, B2 and B3 comparisons to C1, C2, C3 samples, respectively.

The designators (LEFT. MIDDLE, RIGHT) indicate the positions of the choices, from the learner's perspective. The shaded boxes indicate a correct choice, respectively.

	SAMPLE		LEFT	MIDDLE	RIGHT	Differential
			COMPARISONS			Reinforcer
1	C1		B3	B2	B1	R1
2	C2		B1	B2	B3	R2
3	C3		B3	B1	B2	R3
4	C2		B3	B2	B1	R2
5	C1		B2	B3	B1	R1
6	C2		B2	B1	B3	R2
7	C3		B1	B3	B2	R3
8	C2		B2	B3	B1	R2
9	C3		B1	B2	B3	R3
10	C1		B2	B1	B3	R1
11	C2		B3	B1	B2	R2
12	C1		B1	B2	B3	R1
13	C3		B2	B1	B3	R3
14	C1		B1	B3	B2	R1
15	C3		B2	B3	B1	R3
16	C2		B1	B3	B2	R2
17	C1		B3	B1	B2	R1
18	C3		B3	B2	B1	R3

Data Scoring and Compilation

Directions

Make a slash mark under the comparison item each time it appeared in the box when a specific item appeared as the sample (in front of the box). Complete a table for each teaching session conducted.

A-C Relation

	Comparisons		
Samples **A1**	**C1**	**C2**	**C3**
A2			
A3			

C-A Relation

	Comparisons		
Samples **C1**	**A1**	**A2**	**A3**
C2			
C3			

Step 4: Posttests

Directions

Conduct posttests exactly as pretests were conducted, using the same materials.

GENERIC MATCHING-TO-SAMPLE DATA (MTS) SHEET

The letters represent three different items being taught. Each trial has a sample and three comparisons. The sample and the correct comparison may be the same, as in identity matching (reflexivity), or different but related, as in matching a picture to its corresponding spoken name (teaching or symmetry or transitivity).

The designators (LEFT, MIDDLE, RIGHT) indicate the positions of the choices, from the learner's perspective. Samples and comparisons may be any modality (e.g., auditory, visual, tactile, etc.). Regardless, the sample appears above the comparisons.

The shaded boxes indicate a correct choice.

	SAMPLE		LEFT	MIDDLE	RIGHT
				COMPARISONS	
1	A		C	B	**A**
2	B		A	**B**	C
3	C		**C**	A	B
4	B		C	**B**	A
5	A		B	C	**A**
6	B		**B**	A	C
7	C		A	**C**	B
8	B		**B**	C	A
9	C		A	B	**C**
10	A		B	**A**	C
11	B		C	A	**B**
12	A		**A**	B	C
13	C		B	A	**C**
14	A		**A**	C	B
15	C		B	**C**	A
16	B		A	C	**B**
17	A		C	**A**	B
18	C		**C**	B	A

Index

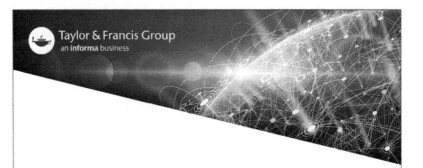

For Product Safety Concerns and Information please contact our EU
representative GPSR@taylorandfrancis.com
Taylor & Francis Verlag GmbH, Kaufingerstraße 24, 80331 München, Germany